Elizabeth Jane Cotton

Young Folks' History of the Middle Ages

Elizabeth Jane Cotton

Young Folks' History of the Middle Ages

ISBN/EAN: 9783337294625

Printed in Europe, USA, Canada, Australia, Japan

Cover: Foto ©Paul-Georg Meister /pixelio.de

More available books at **www.hansebooks.com**

YOUNG FOLKS'

HISTORY OF THE MIDDLE AGES

USED IN 7A GRADE

INDIANAPOLIS PUBLIC SCHOOLS

COMPILED BY

ELIZABETH J. COTTON

INDIANAPOLIS
THE BOWEN MERRILL CO
1898

To Teachers

This work is intended to furnish materials for the foundation of the study of the Middle Ages, and references for more extended reading

MEDIÆVAL HISTORY.

Mediæval History or the History of the Middle Ages is commonly regarded as comprising the events of the 1,000 years from the Fall of Rome (476 A. D.) to the discovery of America in 1492. (See Fall of Rome in "Young Folks' History of Greece and Rome.")

RISE OF THE SARACENS OR ARABS.

Physical Arabia.—We now pass from the forests and rivers of Europe to the sands and deserts in the south of Asia; from a country of clouds, of rains, and of moist vegetation, to one of a burning sun, to the consuming and suffocating simoon, and to dry and aromatic plants. The men dwelling in these two countries are as different as their climates. A people sober in body and mind, of a quick and ardent temperament, seeing nothing but their desired goal and going directly toward it, and accustomed to dash through the desert with the swiftness of an arrow, because of the impossibility of stopping there with impunity and because there was nothing to attract them between the place of departure and that of arrival; a people made either for prompt action or absolute repose—such is the Arab people, and these traits of character are seen in their history.

"The Roman Empire was bounded by the Germans on the north and the Arabs on the south. The former had directed their attacks for the most part toward the Empire of the West and had overthrown it by an invasion prepared and indeed begun long before: the latter emerging suddenly from their deserts had made the Empire of the East their special point of attack, and without overthrowing it entirely, had, as it were, with a single blow of their cimeter, cut off a large portion. It was by astonishing good fortune that the Empire at Constantinople survived these two attacks coming from opposite directions, like an island in the midst of an inundation.

"Arabia, which then appeared for the first time on the stage of history, is a vast peninsula of which some portions are still but little known. It is bordered on the north toward Asia by great deserts, and on the northwest is connected with Africa by the Isthmus of Suez, where the small Peninsula of Sinai projects between the Gulfs of Suez and Akaba. The Peninsula of Arabia forms an imperfect square, with the longest side facing Egypt and Abyssinia across the Red Sea and the Strait of El Mandeb—the shortest side facing Persia, from which it is separated only by the Persian Gulf. The width is very great, especially at the southern end. A chain of mountains, the continuation of the Lebanon range, extends along the Red Sea to Bab-el-Mandeb, the Gate of Tears. Another range borders the Persian Gulf as far as the Strait of Ormuz. These two mountain systems are connected by a line of hills which run from one strait to the other. The inner slopes of these mountains surround a low and arid plateau which forms the center of Arabia, and their outward slopes face the sea and form a girdle of lands, part of which are rich and fertile, and here the heat of the climate is mitigated by the sea breezes, the rains, the water-courses, and the numberless irregularities of the land.

"While the impossibility of permanently settling or of founding anything durable in the interior has always kept up the nomad life, the advantages offered by the coast lands have given birth to fixed institutions and to a civilization which at times has been brilliant enough.

Arabia Divided by the Romans.—"The only knowledge the ancients had of Arabia came through a few scattered Roman expeditions. They divided it into three parts—the Peninsula of Sinai, Arabia Deserta (the deserts which extend from the Red Sea to the Euphrates), and Southern Arabia.

Modern Political Divisions.—"The Arabian geographers, on the other hand, do not include either the peninsula of Sinai or the deserts of Sinai or of the Euphrates in their country, but consider them as lying outside of Arabia. They divided the rest of the peninsula into eight countries: 1, Hedjaz, which borders the Red Sea, southeast of the peninsula of Sinai; 2, Yemen, which lies south of Hedjaz; 3, Hadramaut, on the Indian Sea, at the east of Yemen; 4, Mahrah, at the east of Hadramaut; 5, Oman, between Mahrah and the Persian Gulf and the Indian Ocean; 6, Bahrein, on the Persian Gulf; 7 and 8, Nedjed and Ahkaf, in the interior.

Most Noted Provinces.—"The most fertile of these

provinces is Yemen, which is also well situated for commerce, at the southwestern corner of Arabia, between the Red Sea and the Indian Ocean. This is the country of Aden, of Sana, of the ancient and wonderful Saba, and of Mocha, famous for its coffee. The best known, though not the most fertile, of these provinces is Hedjaz, the country of Mecca and Medina, two cities which ruled all the rest of Arabia through their religious influence, though their situation obliged them to have two ports on the Red Sea, in order to derive means of subsistence from abroad.

Origin of People.—"The Arabs attribute a double origin to their population—a primitive race descended from Shem, according to some, from Ham, according to others, and to descendants from Abraham, who, according to their traditions, in obedience to the commands of God, came to Mecca to found the temple of Kaaba. They say that Abraham lived many years in Hedjaz, and was aided in his divine mission by Ishmael, who was the founder of the Ishmaelites."—*Duruy's Middle Ages.*

"And God said to Abraham, Also of the son of the bondwoman will I make a nation."

"And the lad grew and dwelt in the wilderness and became an archer. And his mother took him a wife out of the land of Egypt."

HAGAR IN THE WILDERNESS.

The morning broke. Light stole upon the clouds
With a strange beauty. Earth received again
Its garment of a thousand dyes; and leaves
And delicate blossoms, and the painted flowers,
And everything that bendeth to the dew

And stirreth with the daylight, lifted up
Its beauty to the breath of that sweet morn.
　All things are dark to sorrow; and the light
And loveliness and fragrant air were sad
To the dejected Hagar. The moist earth
Was pouring odors from its spicy pores,
And the young birds were singing, as if life
Were a new thing to them, but, O! it came
Upon her heart like discord, and she felt
How cruelly it tries a broken heart
To see a mirth in anything it loves.
She stood at Abraham's tent. Her lips were pressed
Till the blood started, and the wandering veins
Of her transparent forehead were swelled out,
As if her pride would burst them. Her dark eye
Was clear and tearless, and the light of heaven
Which made its language legible, shot back
From her long lashes, as it had been flame.
Her noble boy stood by her, with his hand
Clasped in her own, and his round, delicate feet,
Scarce trained to balance on the tented floor,
Sandalled for journeying. He had looked up
Into his mother's face, until he caught
The spirit there, and his young heart was swelling
Beneath his dimpled bosom, and his form
Straightened up proudly in his tiny wrath,
As if his light proportions would have swelled,
Had they but matched his spirit to the man.
　Why bends the patriarch as he cometh now
Upon his staff so wearily? His head
Is low upon his breast, and his high brow
So written with the converse of his God,
Beareth the swollen vein of agony.
His lip is quivering, and his wonted step
Of vigor is not there; and though the morn
Is passing fair and beautiful, he breathes
Its freshness as it were a pestilence.
O, man may bear with sufferings: his heart
Is a strong thing, and godlike in the grasp
Of pain, that wrings mortality; but tear

One chord affection clings to, part one tie
That binds him to a woman's delicate love,
And his great spirit yieldeth like a reed.
  He gave to her the water and the bread,
But spoke no word, and trusted not himself
To look upon her face, but laid his hand
In silent blessing on the fair-haired boy,
And left her to her lot of loneliness.
  Should Hagar weep? May slighted woman turn,
And, as a vine the oak has shaken off,
Bend lightly to her leaning trust again?
O, no! by all her loveliness, by all
That makes life poetry and beauty, no!
Make her a slave; steal from her rosy cheek
By needless jealousies; let the last star
Leave her a watcher by your couch of pain;
Wrong her by petulance, suspicion, all
That makes her cup a bitterness—yet give
One evidence of love, and earth has not
An emblem of devotedness like hers
But, O! estrange her once—it boots not
By wrong or silence, anything that tells
A change has come upon your tenderness—
And there is not a high thing out of heaven
Her pride o'ermastereth not.
  She went her way with a strong step and slow;
Her pressed lip arched, and her clear eye undimmed,
As it had been a diamond, and her form
Borne proudly up as if her heart breathed through.
Her child kept on in silence, though she pressed
His hand till it was pained; for he had caught,
As I have said, her spirit, and the seed
Of a stern nation had been breathed upon.
  The morning passed, and Asia's sun rode up
In the clear heaven, and every beam was heat.
The cattle of the hills were in the shade,
And the bright plumage of the Orient lay
On beating bosoms in her spicy trees.
It was an hour of rest; but Hagar found
No shelter in the wilderness, and on

She kept her weary way, until the boy
Hung down his head, and opened his parched lips
For water; but she could not give it him.
She laid him down beneath the sultry sky,
For it was better than the close hot breath
Of the thick pines, and tried to comfort him;
But he was sore athirst, and his blue eyes
Were dim and bloodshot, and he could not know
Why God denied him water in the wild.
She sat a little longer, and he grew
Ghastly and faint, as if he would have died.
It was too much for her. She lifted him
And bore him further on, and laid his head
Beneath the shadow of a desert shrub;
And, shrouding up her face, she went away,
And sat to watch where he could see her not,
Till he should die; and—watching him, she mourned:

"God stay thee in thine agony, my boy!
I can not see thee die; I can not brook
Upon thy brow to look,
And see death settle on my cradle-joy.
How have I drunk the light of thy blue eye!
And could I see thee die?

"I did not dream of this when thou were straying
Like an unbound gazelle amid the flowers;
Or wearing rosy hours,
By the rich gush of water sources playing,
Then sinking weary to thy smiling sleep,
So beautiful and deep.

"O, no! and when I watched by thee the while,
And saw thy bright lip curling in thy dream,
And thought of the dark stream
In my own land of Egypt, the far Nile,
How prayed I that my father's land might be
An heritage for thee!

"And now the grave for its cold breast hath won thee,
And thy white, delicate limbs the earth will press,
And, O! my last caress

Must feel thee cold, for a chill hand is on thee.
How can I leave my boy, so pillowed there
Upon his clustering hair!"

She stood beside the well her God had given
To gush in that deep wilderness, and bathed
The forehead of her child until he laughed
In his reviving happiness, and lisped
His infant thought of gladness at the sight
Of the cool plashing of his mother's hand.—*N. P. Willis.*

GOD'S GIFTS TO THE ARAB.

[From, Ben-Hur. Read Sheik Ilderim in the Orchard of Palms at Antioch.]

"God gave the first Arab a measureless waste of sand, with some treeless mountains, and here and there a well of bitter waters, and said to him : 'Behold thy country!' And when the poor man complained, the Mighty One pitied him, and said again, 'Be of cheer, for I will twice bless thee above other men.' The Arab heard, and gave thanks, and with faith set out to find the blessings. He traveled all the boundaries first, and failed ; then he made a path into the desert, and went on and on—and in the heart of the waste there was an island of green, very beautiful to see ; and in the heart of the island, lo! a herd of camels, and another of horses! He took them joyfully and kept them with care for what they were— best gifts of God. And from that green isle went forth all the horses of the earth ; even to the pastures of Nesæa they went ; and northward to the dreadful vales perpetually threshed by blasts from the Sea of Chill Winds. Doubt not the story ; or if thou dost, may never amulet have charm for an Arab again."—*Lew Wallace.*

RELIGION OF THE ARABS.

"The Arab population of the north and south formed great powers, and came often into contact, both in peace and war, with foreign powers far and near. They became involved in the affairs of the Roman Empire and of Persia.

"Christianity was preached to them by an envoy, sent by Constantine, but at the beginning of the sixth century they persecuted the new religion, and the Greek emperor induced the king of Abyssinia, who was a Christian, to avenge the wrongs of the cross. The Abyssinians then invaded Yemen (525 A. D.) and, under a viceroy, established their dominion and the Christian religion in this country; and built a church to oppose the Arab one at Mecca. In 575 A. D. the Abyssinians were driven from the country, but only with the assistance of a Persian army, sent by a Persian king, who merely substituted his own dominion for that of the Africans.

"The central region, which had never wielded so great a power, had at least preserved that liberty without which no progress could be made in Arabia. The foreign armies which appeared in the north and south had not penetrated to Hedjaz. More traces of the patriarchal government were found there; the people were divided into tribes composed of a certain number of families, a sheik (lord) at the head of each family; a supreme sheik (emir) at the head of each tribe, which he governed with the advice of the sheiks of the families. In ancient times when a chief took possession of a pasturage he set his pack of hounds barking, and so far as the hound could be heard, so far extended his right of possession. So great simplicity was there in the primitive customs of the people. Nevertheless the population of Hedjaz held a variety and mixture of religious ideas of every sort which prepared them for a brilliant destiny. Being a central state Hedjaz was the meeting-ground of all the others, the point where all intercourse, trade, and ideas converged. Three of the great religions of Asia and Europe, without mentioning idolatry with all its gods, met there: Christianity, which had been carried to the north by the Greeks and to the south by the Abyssinians; Sabianism, brought by the Persians; and, finally, Judaism, which had been introduced everywhere. Three hundred and sixty idols were gathered together in the Kaaba (temple of Mecca), and when Mohammed turned them out there was found to be among the number a Byzantine virgin, painted on a column, holding Christ in her arms. Idolatry was the dominant religion, not the ingenious idolatry of the Greeks who clothed the gods in human form, but the Egyptian idolatry, the worship of animals, of plants, of the gazelle, of the horse, of the camel, of palm-trees, and of rocks. All indeed recognized a supreme god, Allah. The form of this religion had not changed for a long time. As with the Jews, the care of the temple had been given to one chosen family for many years. In 440 A. D. an Ishmaelite family had secured this charge, had rebuilt the temple, and, in a way, founded Mecca and established the principal religious and civil institutions of the Arabs.

Poets.—"The Arabs were poets as well as warriors and merchants; at least they had their bards, like the men of the north, and their feasts, and their poetical contests, such as were held at the Olympic games of the Greeks. Whoever was most successful in moving the souls of the listeners and awakening within them a response, saw his work written in letters of gold on costly canvas and hung in the Kaaba. In this way seven poems have come down to us."—*Duruy.*

Life of Mohammed.—Mohammed was born at Mecca, about the year 570 A. D. His grandfather had defended Mecca against the Abyssinians, and his father was famous for his distribution of soup during a famine. Having lost his father at two months old and his mother at six years of age, he was put under the guardianship of his uncle. Being without fortune he became a camel driver and traveled a great deal, especially in Syria, where he is said to have become intimate with a monk and a Jewish rabbi, who both introduced him to their sacred books, the Old and New Testaments. He fought with bravery in a tribal war, and by his amiable qualities gained the affection of all, and by his probity the name of the trustworthy man. A rich and noble widow took him into her service as director of her commercial affairs, and he served her so well that she married him out of gratitude, although she was forty and he but twenty-five years of age. From that time he was master of a great fortune, and was able to give himself up to his meditations. He often retired to the desert, spending whole nights in revery.

At the age of forty—a mystic number in the east—he

declared that the angel Gabriel had appeared to him in a vision, commissioning him to preach a new faith. He disclosed his projects to his wife, to his cousin Ali, and to his friend Abu Bekr, and declared to them the necessity of bringing the religion of Abraham back to its original purity.

After a time he publicly renounced idol-worship, and proclaimed himself a prophet. Persecution waxed hot, and he was forced to flee for his life. His adherents were alarmed and took refuge in Abyssinia, and he himself retired to the mountains near Mecca.

The chapters of the Koran, which he dictated to his secretary, were written on palm-leaves and on the bones of sheep. It is composed of one hundred and fourteen chapters, which are divided into verses. These verses, containing all the precepts of the Islam morality, are inscribed by the Mohammedans upon the walls of their mosques, on their banners, and on their monuments. The fundamental principle of their dogma is, " God alone is God, and Mohammed is his prophet. It teaches: 'God has been revealed to man by a series of prophets, the last and most perfect of whom is Mohammed; his predecessors are Adam, Noah, Abraham, Moses, and Christ.'" Some of the religious observances are the great annual pilgrimage to Mecca, the five daily prayers, ablutions, either with water, or, if water failed, with the fine sand of the desert, the avoidance of wine and of swine flesh.

When pursued by his enemies, who wished to kill him, Mohammed took refuge in a cave near Mecca; and, in the close of each evening, he received from the son and daughter of Abu Bekr a secret supply of intelligence and food. His enemies diligently explored every haunt in the neighborhood of the city; they arrived at the entrance of the cave, but seeing a spider's web and a pigeon's nest, they passed on in pursuit. "We are only two," said the trembling Abu Bekr. "There is a third," replied the prophet; it is God himself." No sooner was the pursuit abated than the two fugitives issued from the rock and mounted their camels. On the road to Medina, they were overtaken by their pursuers; they redeemed themselves by prayers and promises. In this eventful moment, the lance of an Arab might have changed the history of the world.

The fugitives secured an asylum in Medina, where the new faith spread rapidly and Mohammed found himself at the head of an army. He aroused his followers to go forth to conquer by such precepts as the following:

"Woe to the Mussulman who stays by his fireside instead of going to war; he can not escape death, for the term of his life is fixed. Does he fear the burning heat of the combat? The infernal regions are hotter than the heats of summer. Does he think to turn and flee? Paradise is before him, behind him the flames of the infernal regions. Paradise will be found in the shadow of the crossing of swords." The only choice left the conquered was the Koran, tribute, or death.

The martial apostle fought in person at nine battles or sieges and fifty enterprises of war were achieved in ten years by himself and his lieutenants. The Arab continued to unite the professions of a merchant and a robber; and his petty excursions for the defense or attack of a caravan insensibly prepared his troops for the conquest of

Arabia. From all sides the roving Arabs were allured to the standard of religion and plunder. In three years' time after the taking of Mecca (629) all Arabia lay prostrate at the feet of the prophet. His rule was now firmly established; and an impulse given to the Arabian nation which induced them to invade and enabled them to conquer a large portion of the globe. Mohammed himself did not live to see such mighty conquests achieved, for he died at Medina, A. D. 632.—*Adapted from Duruy and Gibbon.*

CONQUEST OF THE ARABS.

Conquest of Syria.—The *Caliphs*, or successors of Mohammed, rapidly followed up the triumphs of the new faith. Some of the warriors went to the heart of Arabia to put down the false prophets and the tribes who refused to recognize Islamism, others marched against Syria, and others toward the Euphrates and Persia. In six years, Syria was conquered from the Byzantine Greeks.

When besieging *Damascus*, 70,000 men, sent by the Greek emperor, were utterly defeated, and the fugitives from the city were pursued with all the speed of Arab horses, so that they were entirely destroyed. "A second victory in Palestine completed this conquest. A Greek army of considerable size had come out against the Mohammedans; three times they fell back, but each time their wives, who were on horseback, bow in hand, at the rear of the army, sent them back to the combat. The Arabian historians speak of 150,000 enemies slain and 40,000 prisoners."

"*Jerusalem* opened its gates to the Caliph Omar, who came in person to take possession. He was plainly mounted on a rough-haired camel, and carried in front of him, on his saddle, a bag of wheat, a bag of dates, and a leathern bottle of water, and offered to share his repast with all whom he met. He stayed days at Jerusalem in order to regulate the affairs of the country, and to build a mosque, though he allowed the Christians the free exercise of their religion. After Jerusalem, *Aleppo*, and finally *Antioch*, the mighty capital of Syria, surrendered, and the Greek emperor abandoned the country forever (638 A. D.)"

The army which had been sent in the direction of the Euphrates had experienced no less marvelous success. Persia, whose power was already declining, tried in vain with 150,000 soldiers to resist 30,000 Arabs. *Ispahan* was conquered, *Persepolis* sacked, and the king of Persia just escaped being taken prisoner in the midst of his falling palace. He went in search of aid as far as China, but in vain, and was assassinated on the shores of the Oxus (652 A. D.).

Conquest of Egypt.—"Meanwhile Egypt was subjugated. The Arab leader took advantage of the hatred which the Copts felt toward the Greeks, whom they considered as foreigners and heretics. His progress was not checked till he reached *Alexandria*, which held out against him fourteen months. It is generally believed that the Arab leader gave orders to burn the precious library of this rich and learned city. Omar is reported to have said, 'If the manuscripts agree with the Koran, they are useless; if they disagree, they should be destroyed.' Nevertheless the Arabs organized the government with wisdom, substituting a more just system of taxation and reserving one-third of these taxes for the preservation of the canals and ditches.

"*Intestine quarrels* brought the conquest of the Arabs to a halt for the time being. Two great parties arose, those belonging to one gave themselves up to luxury and disobeyed the precepts of their religion ; others by a natural reaction formed the fanatical sects, the puritans of Islamism. The next dynasty was established by rivers of blood. A second and last period of conquests then began."

Eastern Extent.—In the east the Mussulman power extended itself to the limits of Alexander's empire. "The Arabs found at this extreme end of their empire, at Bokhara and Samarcand (707 A. D.), the fruits from the seeds of civilization left there by the Greek conquerors, and they did not allow this growing prosperity to perish.

Attack on Constantinople.—"The Arabs advanced also in the direction of Asia Minor and of Constantinople. So far they had only fought on land, but the Syrian dynasty gave them a maritime power, the elements of which they found in the conquered provinces of Phoenicia and Cilicia."

About fifty years after Mohammed's flight from Mecca, his disciples appeared in arms under the walls of Constantinople. The Greeks had little to hope and their enemies no reason to fear, from the courage and vigilance of the reigning emperor, who disgraced the name of Constantine. Without opposition the Saracens passed through the unguarded channel of the Hellespont and anchored seven miles from the city. The wealth of nations deposited in this well-chosen seat of royalty and commerce seemed about to be distributed among the riders of the desert.

The spirit of the Romans, however, was rekindled by the last danger of their religion and empire. The strength and resources of the Greeks greatly exceeded the estimate of the Arabs. The solid and lofty walls were defended by great numbers of disciplined soldiers who poured torrents of Greek fire from the battlements upon the besiegers. This artificial fire was composed of sulphur, naphtha, and pitch and was hurled from the rampart upon the ships by means of red-hot hollow balls of iron, or blown through copper tubes from the prow of a galley. By the greatest precautions the secret of this composition was confined about four hundred years to the Romans of the East.

After a siege of seven years (668–675) and another of thirteen months, the Arab invasion of Europe in this direction was given up. Their retreat decided that the Eastern Empire should live some centuries longer.— *Adapted from Duruy and Gibbon.*

The Conquest of Northern Africa.—"From Egypt the Saracens bore the triumphant banner of the prophet over northern Africa and by 700 A. D. they had reached the Atlantic. Here, opposite the Canary Islands, their victorious emir, riding out among the waves, lamented that the ocean prevented him from planting the crescent in the unknown kingdoms of the West."—*Quackenbos.*

The deserts of Africa had no terror for the Arabs attended by their faithful camels, but they feared the Roman fleet. Notwithstanding the weakness of the Græco-Roman Empire, Roman soldiers from Constantinople, with Gothic warriors from Italy and Spain, hastened across the Mediterranean Sea to aid in the protection of Carthage and other Roman colonies on the sea-coast. All Europe had begun to feel alarm at the threatening advance of the Saracens, but the combined Christian forces were only able to resist their progress for half a century from their first invasion, 643. By 698 A. D. the dominion of the Arabs was established over the whole length of the African sea-coast by the conquest of Carthage, which was consigned to the flames and has never been rebuilt.

"The ruins of Carthage have perished; and the place might be unknown if some broken arches of an aqueduct did not guide the footsteps of the inquisitive traveler."

After the Greeks were expelled, the country was in constant turmoil owing to the disorderly resistance of the *Berbers* afterwards known as the *Moors*. This tribe of people, called *Berbers* or *Barbarians* by the Romans, inhabited the interior provinces of Northern Africa. They were idolaters at first, but after their last insurrection was quelled in 709, they were thoroughly converted to the faith of the Koran. With the religion they were proud to adopt the language, name, and origin of the Arabs. After this union with the Arabs the Berbers were known as the "Moors."

For a thousand years the history of Northern Africa

had been intertwined with that of Europe and seemed destined to share in the progress of that continent. By this conquest these countries became once more an extension of Asia and have sunk under the yoke of the Arabian prophet. The arts which had been taught by Carthage and Rome were forgotten and five hundred Christian churches were overturned. In no other land has Christianity, once established, been so completely uprooted.—*Adapted from Gibbon and Myers*.

Extent.—The Mohammedan empire now stretched from the Indus to the Atlantic and only the narrow straits of Bosporus and Hercules separated the Moslem dominions from the Christian countries of Europe. The Greek fire had successfully repulsed their attacks at the eastern extremity of the continent and their attention was now directed to the shores of Spain. As early as the first invasion of Africa (643 A. D.) by the Arabs, their piratical squadrons had ravaged the coast of Andalusia. The Goths of Spain had moreover aroused the enmity of the Arabs by sending succor to the inhabitants of Carthage.

Before relating the story of the *conquest of Spain* by the Arabs, we will pause to learn some facts about the physical features of this southwestern peninsula of Europe which is so closely allied to Africa, both in physical characteristics and in its subsequent history.

PHYSICAL SPAIN.

[Read Chapter I, Irving's Alhambra.]

"The surface of Spain is remarkable alike for its striking contrasts and its vast expanses of dreary uniformity. There are mountains rising with Alpine grandeur above the snow line, but often sheltering rich and magnificent valleys at their base. Naked walls of white limestone tower above woods of cork oak and olive. In others, as in the Basque country, in Galicia, and between the head of the Tagus and those of the Guadalquivir, there are extensive tracts of undulating forest-clad hill country. Almost contiguous to these are tracts of level tablelands, some almost inhospitable, and some streaked with canals and richly cultivated, like those of Valencia.

Interior.—"The greater part of the interior of Spain is composed of a table-land bounded by the Cantabrian mountains in the north, and Sierra Morena in the south, and divided into two by a series of mountain ranges stretching from east to west. The northern half of the table-land, made up of the provinces of Leon and Old Castile, has an average elevation estimated at about 2,700 feet, while the southern half is slightly lower. On all sides the table-land as a whole is remarkably isolated. On the side of Portugal the table-land sinks to the sea in a succession of terraces. The communication between the two countries being very difficult, led originally to the separation between them. In modern times it has caused a lack of trade. Even in 1885 not a single railroad entered Portugal north of the Tagus, though one was in course of construction. For the most part there are only bridle-paths across the sierras, and up to the present day not a single railroad crosses the sierras directly. In the mountainous districts, where there are only narrow paths, it is still not uncommon to meet long trains of mules. (See Alhambra, pages 12, 13, 14.)

Rivers.—"The only two important lowland valleys of Spain are of the Ebro and the Guadalquivir.

Climate.—" Four zones are distinguished. The first, that of the table-lands, is distinguished by the greatest extremes. Even in summer the nights are decidedly cool, and it is not a rare thing to see hoar-frost. At Madrid (2150 feet) it regularly freezes hard enough for skating in December and January. The summers are not only extremely warm, but almost rainless, the sea winds being deprived of their moisture by the edge of the plateau. In July and August the plains of Castile are sunburnt wastes; the roads are several inches deep with dust; the leaves of the few trees are withered and discolored. The treeless, almost steppe-like valley of the Ebro acts like a concave mirror, reflecting the sun's rays, and the mountains around prevent the access of the winds. The second zone is the eastern or Mediterranean, where the extremes are less. The southern zone, embracing the whole of Andalusia, has a genuine sub-tropical climate with extremely warm and almost rainless summers and mild winters, the temperature hardly ever sinking below the freezing point. It is said that at Malaga, snow falls only about once in twenty-five years. The winter is the season of brightest vegetation, after the long drought of summer, the surface gets covered once more in late autumn with a fresh green varied with bright colored flowers, and so it remains the whole winter through. The eastern part of this zone is liable to be visited by the scorching sirocco. The fourth zone, that of the north and northwest, is mild and equable. The rains are abundant. Monthly roses bloom in the gardens at Christmas time. (See Irving's "Granada," pages 2 and 3.)

Vegetation and Agriculture.—The vegetation exhibits a variety in keeping with the climate. On the tablelands, where the trees are almost entirely absent, there are tracts of evergreen shrubs, others of thyme, and on some, large thistles abound. The maritime parts of Malaga and Granada present scenes of almost tropical richness and beauty. Evergreen oaks, chestnuts, and conifers abound in the northern maritime provinces and in the south. The pines and firs belong to the slopes of the Sierra Nevada, the cork oaks to the southern provinces, also the date-palm and dwarf-palm. Six steppe regions are counted, La Manche in Castle is one. Along the base of the Sierra Morena, embracing hundreds of square miles, run regular forests of olives. Oranges, excluded from the plateau by the severity of the winter cold, are grown in great quantities on the plains of Andalusia and all around the Mediterranean coast; and figs, almonds, pomegranates and other southern fruits are also grown abundantly in all the warmer parts, the first two even in Central Spain and the more sheltered parts of the northern maritime provinces. In these last, however, the prevailing fruit-trees are those of central Europe, especially the apple. The date-palm is very general in the southeastern half of the kingdom, but cultivated for its fruit in Alicante. Cotton is only grown here and there in the south; sugar-cane is increasing in importance. The mulberry is grown in almost all the provinces, principally along the Mediterranean and above all, in Valencia, the chief seat of the Spanish silk production and manufacture. Of the grains wheat and barley are cultivated in all parts, oats and rye in the higher parts, and corn and rice to some extent, but the latter only in Valencia.—*Compiled from Britannica.*

People.—The Visigoths, who, under the leadership of Alaric, assisted in the downfall of the Roman empire, had found a permanent home in Spain and Southern France. (See "Fall of Rome," in Roman History.) "When they first became masters of Spain, they were a rude tribe of savages without learning or culture." After they had intermingled with the natives (descendants of Roman and Greek colonists) for a century or so they became a refined and polished people, speaking Latin, and trained in letters, law, and religion; and they still remained warlike and manly. But in the course of time they gained possession of the rich valleys of Spain, acquired idle and luxurious habits, spent their lives in drinking, feasting, and dancing, and thus became as weak and helpless as the people of Italy. "Powerful chiefs, with men-at-arms under their command, seized the richest lands, and made the common people till them for their food and clothes. The man who drove the plow was cowed, houseless, hungry, unkempt, filthy, and ignorant. The man who owned the land lived in a splendid castle, with soldiers guarding the gate. He wore clothes of silk and rich stuffs, ate choice foods, drank fine wines, took his siesta in the shade of olive groves, where fragrant flowers perfumed the air, listened to the sweet music of lutes, or lazily watched lovely girls dancing on Persian carpets for his delight.

"At the close of the Gothic period in Spain there is much fable mingled with the history. The Gothic king was named *Roderick;* of that there can be no doubt. He is said to have been brutal, reckless, headstrong, and incapable; of that there is no certainty at all." The country was constantly threatened, as we have before related, by Moors and Arabs from Northern Africa. "To hold them in check, Roderick built forts in Africa, and filled them with fighting men under a captain named Julian." By the treachery of this commander the forts were surrendered to the Arabs and an invitation given to them to despatch a force into Spain to overthrow Roderick.

Arabs Enter Spain.—*Musa,* the chief of the Arabs, delayed till he could consult the caliph; then, receiving a favorable reply, despatched an army of seven thousand men under an officer named *Tarik.* He crossed the Strait of Hercules in 711 and gave it the name of Gibraltar (Djebel-Tarik, Mountain of Tarik.)

"These invaders are called *Moors* because they embarked for Spain from Mauritania, which we call Morocco. They were a mixed race—part Arab and part Berbers, but Musa and Tarik were Arabs, born in Asia. Their complexion was swarthy but not black, and they were fierce, warlike, and unruly in character. They were tireless on the march and fearless in battle; living for a day on a handful of fruit, with a mouthful of water; devoted heart and soul to the Moslem faith, which they believed it to be their duty to spread through the world by fire and sword, they may perhaps remind you of the Carthaginians who spread from the same stock and lived in Northern Africa. They were indeed terrible foes for the weakened Spanish Goths to encounter.

"When Roderick heard of their landing he mustered all the troops he could gather, and marched down to Xeres near Cadiz, with ninety thousand men. It is said that he went into battle in an ivory chariot drawn by two milk-white mules. Though his force far outnumbered that of the Moors, even after the latter had been reinforced, he was defeated after a desperate battle which lasted eight days.

"There is an old Spanish ballad which tells the story of the end of the battle, and describes the despair of Roderick:

> " He climbed into a hill-top,
>   The highest he could see,
> Thence all about of that wide rout
>   His last long look took he:
> He saw his royal banners,
>   Where they lay drenched and torn,
> He heard the cry of victory,
>   The Arabs' shout of scorn.
> ' Last night I was the King of Spain;
>   To-day no king am I.
> Last night fair castles held my train;
>   To-night where shall I lie?
> Last night a hundred pages
>   Did serve me on the knee;
> To-night not one I call my own,
>   Not one pertains to me.
> Oh Death! why now so slow art thou,
>   Why fearest thou to smite?'"

The story is told that Roderick started from his car in the general disorder, and mounted the fleetest of his horses; but he escaped from a soldier's death to perish more ignobly in the waters of Guadalquivir. His body was found, but his crown and his royal robe fell into the hands of the Moors.

"His army scattered; neither officers nor men were true to Roderick. He had taught them to hate him by his cruelties and his folly. The Jews, especially, whom he oppressed, openly took sides with the Moors, in order to be revenged on the Christian oppressors.

"Musa, the chief general of the Moors in Africa, had ordered his lieutenant Tarik, when he left Africa, to give one battle, if he thought it safe, but not to follow up his victory if he won. Musa wanted the glory of conquest for himself. Tarik, looking out for his own glory, chose to disobey. He listened to the advice of Count Julian, whose only hope now was in the ruin of his country, and took advantage of the Spaniards before they had recovered from their astonishment at their first defeat.

"Without an hour's delay, after the battle of Xeres, he marched north, and took city after city. The Spanish spirit had been broken. Malaga made no resistance, Granada was stormed; against Cordova Tarik sent seven hundred cavalry, who found a breach in the walls, and broke into the place."

Toledo, the Gothic capital, was next attacked. There they expected resistance. But the Jews, who had been so cruelly persecuted there, took up arms and opened the gates; the Christian nobles and churchmen fled to the mountains and Tarik found himself in possession of the most splendid and the strongest city of Spain, without striking a blow. "It was there that Musa who had stopped on his way to capture Seville, rejoined his disobedient lieutenant and disgraced him."

(See "A Child's History of Spain," by John Bonner.)

From that time all Spain, save some mountainous regions of the northwest, quickly submitted to the invaders. "Here and there a band of Christians, under a daring leader, would rise against the Moslems, but after a few skirmishes the uprising would be quelled." Yet a spark of the vital flame was still alive; some invincible fugitives preferred a life of poverty and freedom in the valleys of the Asturias, north of the Cantabrian Mountains. There the Christians established a kingdom which in 750 A. D. extended from Galicia to the borders of Navarre and included the mountainous region of Old Castile and Leon.

"This part of Spain is much broken by mountain ranges, and is cold and windy. It is not barren, for it grows wheat, barley, and flax in abundance, and on the mountain slopes the cork-tree flourishes. But the climate is harsher than in the valleys of the South, where the vine, and the orange, and the lemon, and the fig luxuriate in an almost perpetual summer."—*John Bonner.*

Moorish Kingdom in Spain.—The news of the wealth of the new provinces in Spain attracted the Moslems from far and near. Multitudes of colonists from Arabia, Syria, and Northern Africa crowded into the peninsula and fought with each other for the rich valleys. In a short time the provinces of Seville, Cordova, Toledo, and

Granada became Arabic in dress, manners, language, and religion. A Moorish kingdom was thus established in Spain, which existed till the year of the discovery of America (1492).

Moorish Invasion of France (732 A. D.).—Four or five years after the conquest of Spain and one hundred years after the death of Mohammed, the Arabs of Spain —also called Saracens and Moors—crossed the Pyrenees and established themselves in Southern France.

Proceeding northward across the Garonne River, they advanced to the valley of the Loire. Their leader boasted that he would carry the conquests to the Baltic Sea, and that he would not rest until there was not a Christian in Western or Southern Europe. His ambition was to preach in the Vatican, capture Constantinople, and having girdled the Mediterranean with his conquests, to return to Damascus and lay down his victorious sword at the feet of the caliph.

The advance of the Moslem host was viewed with alarm by all Christendom. The Visigoths of Southern France were in too feeble a condition to resist the advance of the Arabs, who swept over the country on their swift chargers. A cry for help reached the Franks, a German tribe living north of the Loire River. During the days of the Roman Empire their home had been along the lower Rhine valley from about where Cologne now stands to the mouth of the river. The Franks did not, like their kinsmen the Goths, Vandals, and Lombards, leave their own country and go roaming over the world in search of new lands. They held what they had and added to them, and this wise conduct enabled them in course of time to become the rulers of France. The Franks had been Christians since the time of their first king, Clovis. (See story of the adoption of Christianity by Clovis; "Zigzag Journey of Northern Lands," and histories.) They had become partially civilized by contact with the Gaulo-Romans, but still liked fighting better than any other employment.—*Adapted*.

Battle of Tours.—When the news of the Arab invasion reached these Franks they were the strongest nation in France and governed by an officer called the Mayor of the Palace. This ruler, Charles, became the man of the hour. Collecting an army of Franks, Gauls, Romans, and Burgundians, he called upon them to strike a blow for God and their country. "He moved as swiftly as the Moors themselves and in a plain near Tours fell upon them like a thunderbolt. The battle lasted only a few hours; the Moslem troops could not stand the mighty shock of the heavy northern infantry; the light African horse reeled under the onset of the great Flemish chargers." "Darkness came on; the Franks slept where they stood and drew up the next morning to begin the battle again, but no enemy appeared. Some Franks were sent to reconnoitre, entered the enemy's camp and penetrated into their tents. But no living man was to be found. (Longfellow's poem "The Day is Done.") The Arabs had decamped silently in the night, and left nearly all their booty behind them. *The Battle of Tours* had saved Europe."—*John Bonner and Miss Yonge*.

Charles, the leader of the *Franks*, received the surname of *Martel*, meaning *hammer*, for the heavy blows he dealt the enemy in this memorable battle. "But for him all Europe might have been Mohammedan, and perhaps—who can say?—you might to this day, at sunset, have been praying to Allah on a prayer rug."—*Bonner.*

Extent of Arabian Empire.—The remnant of the Saracen host made the best of the way back again to Spain, having concluded to postpone the destruction of Christianity till a more convenient season. But that moment was destined never to take place. The limits of the Arabian empire had been reached. The Mohammedans held sway from the Indus to the Pyrenees, but Europe had been saved to Christianity by Greek fire on the east and German valor on the west.

Division of the Mohammedan Empire.—For a century after the death of Mohammed the word of the Caliph of Damascus was law throughout the extent of the empire. No other monarch at that time held such absolute power. In a short time, however, dissension arose, which tore the empire asunder, and three rival caliphs issued commands from three capitals—Bagdad, on the Tigris; Cairo upon the Nile; and Cordova, upon the Guadalquivir. A common language and religion still held them together. All believed in Mohammed as their prophet, and prayed with faces toward Mecca.—*Adapted from Myers.*

Caliphate of Bagdad.—In 762 the capital of the Eastern Empire was changed from Damascus to Bagdad on the Tigris. This celebrated city was built around a hill which was crowned by the pavilion of the caliphs. It was defended from attacks without by a brick enclosure, fortified with 163 towers. Immense sums were spent on its decoration. In that stronghold of despotism the caliphs of the East followed in the steps of the Persian kings, accumulated vast wealth and lived in the luxury of their pompous courts. A prime minister called the Vizier and officers of all kinds relieved the sovereign from all cares of government, but they also separated him from his subjects. "One caliph spent twelve million dollars in a single pilgrimage to Mecca. What had become of Omar with his bag of dates and his leather bottle of water?"—*Adapted from Duruy*.

Haroun-al-Raschid.—The most noted of the Caliphs of Bagdad was Haroun-al-Raschid (the Just), contemporary of Charlemagne and hero of the "Arabian Nights." He made eight invasions of the Eastern Empire, forbade the Greeks ever to rebuild the town of Heraclius on the Pontus, which he had destroyed, and laid upon them a tribute which they were obliged to pay in money stamped with his image. But even while he was waging war on them, he borrowed from their science and their books, and made them popular among the Arabs by the protection he accorded to scholars. His son founded many schools and spent enormous sums in the encouragement of science and literature.—*Adapted from Duruy*. (See "Arabian Nights.")

Creation of the Turkish Guard.—In the ninth century, the caliph which followed Haroun-al-Raschid and his son, although victorious in the wars with the Greek Empire, prepared the way for the fall of the Arabian Empire by forming a guard of 50,000 Turkish slaves, bought in Tartary south of the Altai Mountains. The original Turks were a Mongol race from the high plateaus of Central Asia. As the Germans before this pressed into the Roman Empire so now the Turks invaded the Arab Empire. The body-guard of Turks proved as fatal to the Arabs as the Goths did to the Romans. They proved masters rather than slaves. This body of soldiers disposed, at their will, of the throne and the lives of the caliphs. In the midst of this anarchy the Caliphate of Bagdad fell to pieces. Independent dynasties were springing up on every side, founded generally by the Turks who had been made governors of provinces. In this way the Turks were introduced little by little into Southwestern Asia. As the Teutons took the religion of the Romans, so also the Turks accepted the faith of the Arab and became the ardent supporters of the Koran. About the time of the Norman conquest of England, the Turks conquered Bagdad, and in 1076 they seized Jerusalem, where their brutal treatment of the Christian pilgrims caused the Crusades.—*Adapted from Duruy.*

Arabs in Africa.—Africa soon broke away from the Caliphate of Bagdad. The caliphs were masters of the Mediterranean in the ninth and tenth centuries, establishing themselves in Corsica, Sardinia, and Sicily, besides making several attacks on Italy. To guard against them Pope Leo IV. enclosed the neighborhood of the Vatican with a rampart. The Fatimites, the greatest of the Mussulman dynasties in Africa, pretending to descend from Ali, built Cairo, made their residence there and extended their rule over all Northern Africa, Syria, and even over Bagdad for a brief time. This dynasty brought prosperity to Egypt and gained wealth in return. They built superb mosques and made Cairo a center of science and literature, as Bagdad was in the East and Cordova in the West.—*Adapted from Duruy.* (See Crusades.)

Arabian Civilization—*Language.*—The Arab language is exceedingly rich in certain respects. The Arab poets had an inexhaustible supply of synonyms to express common objects. They boasted of having eighty different terms to express honey, 200 for serpent, 500 for lion, 1,000 for camel, and about 4,000 to express the idea of misfortune. The Arabian poet possessed an extraordinary memory that enabled him to make use of such a multitude of words. One of them, Hammad, offered one day to recite to the caliph consecutively 100 poems of 20 to 100 verses each, and the auditor was more quickly tired than the reciter.

Sciences.—"As early as the first half of the ninth century, two astronomers of Bagdad measured, in the plains near the Red Sea, a degree of the meridian." A more exact calculation of the obliquity of the ecliptic, a more precise knowledge of the difference between the solar year and the sidereal year were discoveries of the Arabs. Samarcand, long before Europe, had a fine observatory. They applied the pendulum to the reckoning of time; employed in mathematics the Indian mode of numeration; gave to algebra and trigonometry their modern forms. It is possible that we inherit from them the mariner's compass and gunpowder, which may have been borrowed from the Chinese. Europe owes to them the use of linen paper. They excelled in the practice of medicine; taught us the process of distillation and the use of rhubarb; they discovered alcohol, the use of senna, camphor, mercury, syrups, etc. A physician refused to go from Bagdad to Bokhara at the invitation of the sultan, on the plea that his private library would make four hundred camel-loads. Great public libraries were collected, one at Cairo being said to number 100,000 volumes and the Spanish 600,000.—*Adapted from Duruy.*

Architecture.—"Of the fine arts, they cultivated architecture alone, as the law of their religion forbade the representation of animal life, and so cut off the possibility of sculpture and painting." The principal element of their architecture, the pointed or horseshoe arch borne on pillars, was not their own invention, but was borrowed from the Byzantine. They supplied the places of painted or sculptured figures in their ornamentation, by arabesques which were originally inscriptions with meaning, but later became merely combinations of lines borrowed from the Arabic letters. These arabesques form the rich designs we admire in the carpets and stuffs of the East. The Arabian mosques and palaces are famed for the magnificence and luxury of the interiors, and the profusion of basins and fountains of gold and precious stones, which they obtained from the East and the mines of Southern Spain. One of the most magnificent monuments of this kind was the famous mosque at Cordova, with its 1,093 marble columns and its 4,700 lamps; another was the palace of Al-Tehra, built upon the banks of the Guadalquivir, where a jet of mercury fell sparkling into a shell of porphyry. The Alhambra, at once a palace and a fortress, can still be seen and admired at Granada, and many parts of it, especially the

Court of Lions, are models of architectural beauty and splendor."—*Adapted from Duruy.*

Irrigation.—"No one knew so well as those inhabitants of the desert how to make the best use of water in the work of cultivation under a burning sun. The system of irrigation instituted by them, and still preserved in the plain of Valencia, the garden of Spain, might serve as a model to the agriculturists of our own times. When they went to the great Roman cities and became acquainted with works of industry, they developed great skill as artisans. The reputation of Toledo for its arms, Granada for its silks, and Cordova for its harnesses, saddles, and leather goods, spread throughout Europe, and these products of infidel industry brought the highest prices. Spain especially profited by this time of splendor, as she was more peaceful than the East during the first centuries of the caliphate."—*Duruy.* (See Luxury of Moors, Irving's "Granada.")

Granada.—"This renowned kingdom, situated in the southern part of Spain, and washed on one side by the Mediterranean Sea, was traversed in every direction by sierras or chains of lofty, rugged mountains, naked, rocky, and precipitous, rendering it almost impregnable, but locking up within their sterile embraces deep, rich, and verdant valleys of prodigal fertility.

"In the center of the kingdom lay its capital, the beautiful city of Granada, sheltered, as it were, in the lap of the Sierra Nevada, or Snowy Mountains. Its houses, seventy thousand in number, covered two lofty hills with their declivities, and a deep valley between them, through which flowed the Darro. The streets were narrow, as is usual in Moorish and Arab cities, but there were occasionally small squares and open places. The houses had gardens and interior courts, set out with orange, citron, and pomegranate trees, and refreshed by fountains, so that as the edifices ranged above each other up the sides of the hills, they presented a delightful appearance of mingled grove and city. One of the hills was surmounted by the Alcazaba, a strong fortress, commanding all that part of the city; the other by the Alhambra, a royal palace and warrior castle, capable of containing within its alcazar and towers a garrison of forty thousand men; but possessing also its harem, the voluptuous abode of the Moorish monarchs, laid out with courts and gardens, fountains and baths, and stately halls, decorated in the most costly style of Oriental luxury. Such was its lavish splendor that even at the present day, the stranger, wandering through its silent courts and deserted halls, gazes with astonishment at gilded ceiling and fretted domes, the brilliancy and beauty of which have survived the vicissitudes of war and the silent dilapidation of ages.

"The city was surrounded by high walls, three leagues in circuit, furnished with twelve gates, and a thousand and thirty towers. Its elevation above the sea, and the neighborhood of the Sierra Nevada, crowned with perpetual snows, tempered the fervid rays of summer; so that, while other cities were panting with the sultry and stifling heat of the dog-days, the most salubrious breezes played through the marble halls of Granada.

"The glory of the city, however, was its vega or plain, which spread out to a circumference of thirty-seven leagues, surrounded by lofty mountains, and was proudly compared to the famous plain of Damascus. It was a vast garden of delight, refreshed by numerous fountains, and by the silver windings of the Xenil. The labor and ingenuity of the Moors had diverted the waters of the river into thousands of rills and streams, and diffused them over the whole surface of the plain. Indeed, they had wrought up this happy region to a degree of wonderful prosperity, and took a pride in decorating it, as if it had been a favorite mistress. The hills were clothed with orchards and vineyards, the valleys embroidered with gardens, and the wide plains covered with waving grain. Here were seen in profusion the orange, the citron, the fig, and pomegranate, with great plantations of mulberry trees, from which was produced the finest silk. The vine clambered from tree to tree; the grapes hung in thick clusters about the peasant's cottage, and the groves were rejoiced by the perpetual song of the nightingale. In a word, so beautiful was the earth, so pure the air, and so serene the sky of this delicious region, that the Moors imagined the paradise of their prophet to be situated in that part of the heaven which overhung the kingdom of Granada."—*Irving*.

Palace of the Alhambra.—"The Alhambra was the royal abode of the Moorish kings, where, surrounded with the splendor and refinements of Asiatic luxury, they held dominion over what they vaunted as a terrestrial paradise, and made their last stand for empire in Spain. The royal palace forms but a part of the fortress, the walls of which, studded with towers, stretch irregularly round the whole crest of a hill, a spur of the

Sierra Nevada or Snowy Mountains, and overlook the city. Externally it is a rude congregation of towers and battlements, with no regularity of plan nor grace of architecture, and giving little promise of the grace and beauty which prevail within. * * * The great vestibule or porch of the gate is formed by an immense Arabian arch, of the horseshoe form, which springs to half the height of the tower. On the keystone of this arch is engraven a gigantic hand. Within the vestibule on the keystone of the portal is sculptured, in like manner, a gigantic key. * * * There was a tradition handed down from the oldest inhabitants that the hand and the key were magical devices on which the fate of the Alhambra depended. The Moorish king who built it was a great magician and laid the whole fortress under a magic spell. By this means it had remained standing for several years, in defiance of storms and earthquakes, while almost all other buildings of the Moors had fallen to ruin and disappeared. This spell, the tradition went on to say, would last until the hand on the outer arch should reach down and grasp the key, when the whole pile would tumble to pieces and all the treasures buried beneath it by the Moors would be revealed. * * *"

The Court of Lions.—" Passing under a Moorish archway, we entered the renowned Court of Lions. No part of the edifice gives a more complete idea of its original beauty than this, for none has suffered so little from the ravages of time. In the center stands the fountain famous in song and story. The alabaster basins still shed their diamond drops; the twelve lions which support them and give the court its name still cast forth crystal streams as in the days of Boabdil. The lions, however, are unworthy of their fame, being of miserable sculpture, the work probably of some Christian captive. The court is laid out in flower-beds, instead of its ancient and appropriate pavement of tiles or marble. The alteration, an instance of bad taste, was made by the French when in possession of Granada. Round the four sides of the court are light Arabian arcades of filagree work, supported by slender pillars of white marble, which, it is supposed, were originally gilded. The architecture, like that in most parts of the interior of the palace, is characterized by elegance rather than grandeur, bespeaking a delicate and graceful taste, and a disposition to indolent enjoyment. When one looks upon the fairy traces of the peristyles and the apparently fragile fretwork of the walls, it is difficult to believe that so much has survived the wear and tear of centuries, the shocks of earthquakes, the violence of war, and the quiet, though no less baneful, pilferings of the tasteful traveler. It is almost sufficient to excuse the popular tradition, that the whole is protected by a magic charm. * * *"

"An abundant supply of water, brought from the mountains by old Moorish aqueducts, circulates throughout the palace, supplying its baths and fish-pools, sparkling in jets within its halls or murmuring in channels along the marble pavements. When it has paid its tribute to the royal pile, and visited its gardens and parterres, it flows down the long avenue leading to the city, tinkling in rills, gushing in fountains, and maintaining a perpetual verdure in those groves that embower and beautify the whole hill of the Alhambra."

"An Arab inscription says: 'How beautiful is this garden, where the flowers of earth vie with the stars of heaven! What can compare with the vase of yon alabaster fountain filled with the crystal water? Nothing but the moon in her fullness shining in the midst of an unclouded sky.'

"Those who have sojourned in the ardent climate of the South can appreciate the delights of an abode combining the breezy coolness of the mountain with the freshness and verdure of the valley. While the city below pants with the noontide heat, and the parched vega trembles to the eye, the delicate airs from the Sierra Nevada play through these lofty halls, bringing with them the sweetness of the surrounding gardens. Everything invites to that indolent repose—the bliss of southern climates; and while the half-shut eye looks out from shaded balconies upon the glittering landscape, the ear is lulled by the rustling of groves and the murmur of running streams."—*Irving*.

THE ALHAMBRA.

Lonely and still are now thy marble halls,
  Thou fair Alhambra! There the feast is o'er,
And with the murmur of thy fountain falls
  Blend the wild tones of minstrelsy no more.

Hushed are the voices that in years gone by
  Have mourned, exulted, menaced through thy towers.
Within thy pillared courts the grass waves high,
  And all uncultured bloom thy fairy bowers.

Unheeded there the flowering myrtle blows,
  Through tall arcades unmarked the sunbeam smiles,
And many a tint of softened radiance throws
  O'er fretted walls and shining peristyles.

And well might Fancy deem thy fabrics lone,
 So vast, so silent, and so wildly fair,
Some charmed abode of beings all unknown,
 Powerful and viewless, children of the air.

For there no footstep treads the enchanted ground;
 There not a sound the deep repose pervades,
Save winds, and founts, diffusing freshness round,
 Through the light domes and graceful colonnades.

For other tones have swelled those courts along.
 In days romance yet fondly loves to trace—
The clash of arms, the voice of choral song,
 The revels, combats of a vanquished race;

And yet awhile at Fancy's potent call
 Shall rise that race, the chivalrous, the bold,
Peopling once more each fair, forsaken hall
 With stately forms—the knights and chiefs of old.
—*Mrs. Hemans.*

RISE OF THE TEUTONIC NATIONS.

When the Roman Empire fell the barbarians of the South and North rose to assert their influence as nations. On the preceding pages we have traced the rise and decline of the power of those fearless riders of the desert, the Arabs; now we will return to view the progress of those Teutonic, or Germanic people, who left their native forest and shattered the Roman Empire into fragments, then, upon the ruins of the civilization they had overthrown, laid the foundation of the modern nations. (See page 322 Barnes.)

Physical Germany.—Germany is divided into two distinct portions; the northern and larger part is a uniform plain, while South and Central Germany are very much diversified in scenery. It possesses large plateaus, such as that of Bavaria, which stretches away from the foot of the Alps, fertile low plains like that intersected by the Rhine, mountain chains and isolated groups of mountains comparatively low in height.

Bavarian Plateau.—Bavaria is the only division of the country that includes within it any part of the Alps. This plateau, having an average height of 1,800 feet, slopes northward from the Bavarian Alps to the Bavarian Forests (Bayerisher Wald), which must be regarded as a branch of the Bohemian Forest (Bohmisher Wald). It is watered by the Danube and its tributaries, the Inn, Isar, and Lech. The region is not very fertile, and many portions of it are covered with moors and swamps. To the westward low plateaus occupy the area between the Main and Neckar.

Southwest Germany.—"The Schwazwald (Black Forests) are a range of hills lying east of the upper Rhine valley in Baden, whose southern heights decline to the valley of the Rhine above Basle and to the Jura. On the north the range passes into the plateau, which slopes to the mouth of the Neckar. The summits of the Black Forests are round and covered with wood, the highest being 4,902 feet.

Upper Rhine Valley.—"The valley of the upper Rhine extends 180 miles from south to north, and with a width of only twenty to twenty-five miles. In the upper parts the Rhine is rapid, and therefore navigable with difficulty. This explains why the towns there are not along the banks of the river, but some five to ten miles off. The western boundary of this valley is formed by the Vosges Mountains. These hills are bordered on the west by the high plain of Lorraine and the coal fields of the Saar River, a tributary of the Moselle. The larger half of Lorraine belongs to France, but the German half, obtained in 1871, possesses great mineral wealth in its rich layers of ironstone and its coal fields. The hills south of Mainz (Mayence), on the west of the Rhine, are mostly covered by vineyards. On the east from Mainz to Coblenz the hills are noted for mineral springs and for the vineyards which produce the best Rhine wines. To the north of the hills, east of Cologne and Dusseldorf, lies the great coal basin of Westphalia, the largest in Germany.

In Central Germany lies Thuringia, a province consisting of a wooded ridge and an elevated plain to the north. This plateau is bounded on the north by the Hartz Mountains, an insolated group rich in minerals. East of Thuringia lies Saxony, noted for its metals and building stone. In Silesia are minor coal-fields.

Northern Plain.—The north German plain is not absolutely uniform, having a range of low hills in the south. In general the soil can not be called fertile, the cultivation nearly everywhere requiring severe and constant labor. Long stretches of ground are covered by moors, and there turf-cutting forms the principal occupation of the inhabitants. Tracts along the Elbe, and the marsh lands on the west coast of Hanover, Oldenburg, and East Frisia, which, within the last two centuries, the inhabitants have reclaimed from the sea by immense dikes, are districts of the utmost fertility.

Climate.—It is regarded as intermediate between the Oceanic and Continental climates of western and eastern

Europe. It has nothing in common with the Mediterranean climate; in the west no chain of hills intercepts the warmer and moist winds which blow from the Atlantic, and these influence at times even the eastern regions of Germany. The warmest districts of the German Empire are the northern parts of the Rhine plain, from Carlsruhe downwards, also the valley of the Neckar, Main, and Moselle. Hence the vine is cultivated in these districts. The rainfall is greatest in the Bavarian tableland and in the hilly region of western Germany; also the coast region of Hamburg and Bremen. The grape district is famous for the scarcity of rain. The provinces of central and southeastern Germany are to be classed among the more arid regions.

Coast and Islands.—The coasts of Germany are shallow and deficient in natural ports, except on the east of Schleswig-Holstein, where wide bays encroach upon the land, giving access to the largest vessels, so that a great harbor for men-of-war has been constructed at Kiel. A canal now connects the North Sea and the Baltic. All the important trading ports are river ports, such as Bremen, Hamburg, Stettin, Dantzic, Konigsburg. A great difference is to be remarked between the coasts of the North Sea and the Baltic. On the former, where the sea has broken the ranges of dunes formed in bygone times and divided them into separate islands, the main-land has to be protected by massive dikes, while the Frisian Islands are being gradually washed away by the waters. Sands surround the whole coast of the North Sea to such an extent that entrance to the ports is not practicable without the aid of pilots. Heligoland, which has belonged to England since 1814, is a rocky island; but it also has been considerably reduced by the sea. The tides rise to the height of twelve or thirteen feet in the Jahde Bay and six or seven feet at Hamburg. The coast of the Baltic, on the other hand, possesses few islands. It has no extensive sands, though, on the whole, very flat. The Baltic has no perceptible tides, and a greater part of its coast line is, in winter, covered with ice, which also so blocks up the harbors that navigation is interrupted for several months in the year.

Minerals.—Germany abounds in iron ore, but the deposits are far from the coal, as in Hesse, Thuringia, Bavaria, Wurtemburg. Since the incorporation of Lorraine, in 1871, to the German Empire, the pig-iron production of Germany exceeds that of France. The greatest advance in production of steel has been made. The celebrated Krupp works in Westphalia have for a considerable time supplied many European states with caststeel guns. Germany stands second to Great Britain in manufacture of machines and engines. In agricultural machinery, it can not compete with England.

Germany produces more copper and silver than any other European state. (Zinc and salt, page 112 geography).

Cotton Manufacture.—As the cotton manufacture is pursued largely in Alsace, more than two million spindles being employed there, since 1871 the production of cotton fabrics in Germany exceeds that of France.

Woolen and Worsted.—In this class of manufactures Germany is far behind France. First of all, the home production of wool is not sufficient. Alsace and Saxony are two of the centers of the manufacture of woolen cloth.

Linen, Hemp and Jute.—Although linen was formerly one of Germany's most important articles of manufacture, she is now left far behind in this industry, not only by Great Britain and France, but also by Austria-Hungary. Hand-loom weaving is practiced all over Germany, but centers principally in Saxony, Silesia, and Westphalia.

Army and Navy.—Every German capable of bearing arms must serve in the standing army for seven years. Three of the seven must be spent in active service and the remainder in the reserve. For five years more he forms a part of the landwehr.—*Adapted from Britannica.*

Early German Civilization.—These German tribes called themselves *Deutsch* or the *people*. In time they came to be called *Ger-men* or *war-men*. Their native country south of the Baltic Sea was "full of marshes and forests in which large rivers rose and straggled, widening down to their swampy mouths. Bears and wolves, elks and buffaloes, ran wild, and were hunted by the men of the German tribes." (See page 322 Barnes.)

These men, our German ancestors, were a gigantic white-skinned, blue-eyed, yellow-haired race.

"They lived in villages of rude huts, surrounded by lands to which all had a right in common, and where they grew their corn and fed their cattle. Their wives were much more respected than those of other nations; they were usually strong, brave women, able to advise their husbands and to aid them in the fight; and the authority of fathers and mothers over their families was supreme. The men were either freemen or nobles, and they had slaves, generally prisoners or the people of conquered countries. The villages were formed into what was called hundreds, over which, at a meeting of the freemen from all of them, a chief was elected from among the nobles; and many of the tribes had kings," who were thought to be descended from the great god Woden. (Read Saxon Boy in "Ten Boys" by Jane Andrews; Miss Yonge's History of Germany.)

The Franks.—This German tribe, as we have already related, extended their dominion westward from the Rhine across northern France. They were destined to give a new name to Gaul and form the nucleus of the French nation. After the downfall of Rome, Clovis, then chief of the Franks, extended his authority over the greater part of Gaul.

The Franks Become Christians.—Clovis was a heathen but he married a Burgundian maiden, named Clothilda who was a Christian. He allowed her to worship God in the Christian churches which had been erected by the Romans and still stood throughout Gaul. In the year 496 A. D. the Germans came with a great army across the Rhine. Clovis with his army of Franks met the invaders near Strassburg (some authorities say near Cologne). A severe battle followed. Clovis was hard pressed and cried aloud, " Christ, whom Clothilda calls the true God, I have called on my own gods and they help me not! Send help and I will own thy name." The tide of battle turned as by a miracle and the king with 3,000 of his warriors received baptism at

Rhiems on Christmas Day, 496.—*Adapted from Miss Yonge and Butterworth.*

The Strassburg Cathedral.—That great monument of faith, the Strassburg cathedral, was founded by Clovis. "Its history is that of Germany. It grew with the German empire and has shared all its triumphs and reverses. In the tenth century it was burned, in the eleventh plundered; and five years after it was nearly demolished by lightning. It was after the last calamity that the present structure was begun.

"At one time a hundred thousand men were employed upon it; can we wonder that it is colossal? The giant grew. In 1140, 1150, and 1176 it was partly burned, but it rose from the flames always more great, lofty, and splendid.

"Indulgences were offered to donors and workmen; to contributors of all kinds. Men earned or thought they earned, their salvation by adding their mites to the spreading magnificence. In 1303, it is said that all the peasants of Alsace might be seen drawing stone into Strassburg for the cathedral. Master builder succeeded master builder,—died,—but the great work went on.

"In the French Revolution the Jacobins tore from the cathedral the statues of two hundred and thirty saints; but it was still a city of saints in stone and marble. In 1870, in the Franco-Prussian war, its roof was perforated with shells, and on the 25th of August it burst into flames and it was telegraphed over the world that the great cathedral was destroyed. But it stands to-day, majestic, regal, and beautiful, its spire piercing the sky." Its windows burn with color and seem to hang in the air amid the shadows of the lofty walls. They represent scriptural subjects.

"The cathedral is the wonder of the city. The excursionist thinks of but little else during his stay there. Wherever he may be, the gigantic church is always in view. He beholds it towering above all." The wonderful clock in its steeple seems but a toy in this monument of art.—*Butterworth's "Zigzag Journey of N. Lands."* (See description of clock in Stoddard Pictures.)

Kings of the Franks.—"Clovis was the first Frankish chief who really made a home of Gaul, or who wore a purple robe and a crown like a Roman emperor. He made his chief home at Paris, where he built a church on the little island in the Seine, in honor of the Blessed Virgin. Though he had become a Christian, he was still a fierce, violent savage, who did many cruel things.

"The Frank kingdom was only the north part of the country above the Loire. In the south, where the Romans had had possession so much longer, and built so many more walled towns, the Franks never really lived." They used to rush down and plunder the country round about; but then the townsmen shut themselves in, closed their gates, and strenghened their walls. The Franks having no machines to batter the walls, and no patience for a blockade, went home again with only the spoil of the country round. In these towns of the south the people called themselves Roman citizens still, and each place was governed by the old Roman law. Many Latin speaking Gauls lived in northern France as well, and were respected by the Franks for their knowledge and skill. "The clergy, too, were most all Gauls; and now the Franks were Christians in name at least, they seldom damaged a church or broke into a monastery. When Clovis died his four sons divided the kingdom among themselves. Not that they really governed, only each had a strong box filled with gold and jewels, and they were leaders when the Franks went out to plunder in the southern lands of Provincia and Aquitaine."—*Miss Yonge's " Pop. Hist. of France."*

The Do-nothing Kings.—The line of kings who followed the sons of Clovis were called the long-haired kings. They hardly attended at all to the affairs of their kingdoms, but only amused themselves in their palaces at Soissons or Paris, thus obtaining the name of the do-nothing kings. The affairs of the kingdom fell into the hands of the king's steward who was called the *Major Domi* or *Mayor of the Palace.*" Under the foolish do-nothing kings the Mayor of the Palace came to be a much greater man than the king himself. *Charles Martel* who repulsed the Saracens at the battle of Tours was one of these mayors.

Pepin the Short, the son of Charles Martel, wielded the same power as his father but soon coveted the title of king. After obtaining the consent of the Pope, he sent the last of the do-nothing monarchs, shorn of his long, yellow, royal locks, into a monastery and was himself anointed King of the Franks by St. Boniface, the great missionary-bishop. Pepin was a great improvement on the do-nothing monarchs, but even he did not cause his sons to learn to write, looking upon that accomplishment as belonging to the clergy.—*Adapted.*

Beginning of the Papal States.—At the request of the Pope, who was hard pressed by the Lombards, Pepin invaded Italy, humbled their king, and laid the keys of their conquered cities on the tomb of St. Peter as a gift to the Holy See. This was the beginning of the Pope's temporal authority, that is, holding lands like a king or prince.—*Adapted from Miss Yonge.*

Life of Charlemagne.—Pepin's son, Charlemagne, united the fragments of the old Roman Empire and was the greatest ruler of the Middle Ages. The Franks called him "Carl de Grösse;" the Latin name was *Carolos Magnus* and this has become in French *Charlemagne.*

Character and Dress.—"This noted king was, like his German ancestors, a giant in stature and strength, of commanding presence, and proficient in all manly exercises."—*Quackenbos.* "He was a powerful warrior, and very fond of hunting but preferred swimming to anything else. Nobody could dive or swim like him; and he used to take large parties to bathe with him, so that a hundred men were sometimes in the river at once."—*Miss Yonge.* He wore the simple Frankish dress, which was "a shirt and drawers of linen, over them a tunic bordered with silken fringe, stockings fastened with narrow bands, and shoes. In winter, a coat of otter or martin fur covered his shoulders and breast. Over all he wore a long blue mantle." "He was always girded with his sword, which became so famous that it received the name of *Joyeuse*, whose hilt was of gold and silver, his girdle being also of gold. Upon solemn festive occasions this sword was replaced by one enriched with precious stones."—*Lydia H. Farmer's "Boy's Book of Famous*

Rulers." After he became emperor he assumed the royal purple but twice. He then wore a dress "embroidered with gold and his shoes adorned with jewels. His mantle was fastened with a brooch of gold and he wore upon his head a glistening diadem of gold and gems."—*Lydia Farmer.* He discouraged useless extravagance in his courtiers and when he saw a young noble overdressed, he enjoyed taking him on a long muddy ride in the rain.

Unlike his German ancestors he was strictly temperate in food and drink. Drunkenness, the greatest vice of his race, he abhorred.

The domestic life of this great man was not at all in keeping with the majesty and goodness and uprightness of his public life. He quarreled with his brother and drove him into exile, where he soon died. He quarreled with his wife, the daughter of the king of Lombardy, and sent her back to her father.

Conquests.—The king of Lombardy, enraged at having his daughter thrown back on his hands, declared war. Charlemagne marched into Italy with a large army, drove the Lombards into Pavia and besieged them there. "It was a long siege, and Charlemagne had a chapel set up in his camp to keep Christmas in ; but for Easter he went to Rome, and was met a mile off by all the chief citizens and scholars carrying palm branches in their hands, and as he mounted the steps to St. Peter's church the Pope met him, saying, 'Blessed is he that cometh in the name of the Lord.' He prayed at all the chief churches in Rome, and then returned to Pavia, which was soon after taken. He then took the title of king of the Franks and the Lombards, and put the iron crown of Lombardy on his head."—*Miss Yonge.*

The Saxons.—All the German tribes except the Saxons were subjects of the king of the Franks. "These Saxons—the ancestors of the English and Germans of to-day—were then a tribe, or a band of tribes, settled in the country that is now northern Germany, between the Rhine and the Elbe, and stretching south as far as Bohemia. They lived either in the woods, so dense that it is said a squirrel could travel twenty miles, leaping from branch to branch, without touching the ground, or in vast prairies which were often water-soaked in summer and frozen over in winter. They had never been conquered and had never become Christians; they were as brave and as fierce and as savage as they had been when they defied Cæsar to invade their country. From France missionaries had gone to convert them, and had barely escaped with their lives." Charlemagne undertook the conversion of these Saxons by force. "To be near at hand for this work, he moved his court from Paris to Aix-la-Chapelle, which is near the Rhine in Germany." He then marched against the Saxons and overthrew their idol, which was a huge man with a balance in one hand and a flag in the other; on his arm hung a buckler, with a lion on it. The destruction of this statue so exasperated the Saxons that they rose again and again, flying to their wooded heights to gain breath, and renewing the war just when they were least expected. "They had an exceedingly brave and ingenious chief named Witikind, who fought year after year, and was almost always beaten, yet was

never conquered. Charlemagne tried every device of war with small success." He once beheaded 4,500 prisoners to strike terror to their friends. "Again he would surround Saxon settlements and transplant every one—men, women, and children—to some distant part of France. But those who remained still continued to resist." Vast numbers of them were baptized in the Elbe and Weser rivers. They did not object so much to baptism, the meaning of which they probably did not understand. "They came to be baptized not once but many times, because they were pleased with the white robes provided them. But the baptized Saxons fought as fiercely against the Franks as those who had not undergone the operation. The war lasted thirty-three years. It was not till 805 that Charlemagne could say that it was positively ended, that the Saxons were finally subdued, and that his empire extended from the Atlantic Ocean to the Elbe and almost to the Oder."
—"*Child's Hist. of France*," *Bonner*.

Crusade Against Saracens.—While this Saxon war was in progress, Charlemagne undertook a war against the Moors in Spain. " In 778 he crossed the Pyrenees and overran the country as far as the Ebro, where the Arabs offered him large gifts of gold and jewels if he would return without touching their splendid cities in the South. He consented, but as he was returning the wild Basque people of the mountains fell upon the rear guard of his army in one of the passes and plundered the baggage, slaying some of his bravest leaders. Among them was the famous Roland, concerning whom wonderful stories are told. It is said that he blew a blast on his bugle with his last strength to warn Charlemagne who was far in the front. "Another legend makes him to have possessed herculean strength, in proof of which a great cleft is shown in the Pyrenees said to have been made by one stroke of his sword, and it bears the name of the " La Breche De Roland."—*Adapted from L. H. Farmer's " Boys' Book of Famous Rulers."*

Campaigns.—Charlemagne made war successfully on all the peoples whom his predecessors had fought. He made fifty-two expeditions, the chief of which were against the Lombards, the Saracens, and Saxons, and were for the most part led by Charlemagne himself.

Extent of Empire.—"His lands stretched from the Baltic Sea to the Mediterranean and the Ebro, from the Bay of Biscay to the borders of the Huns and the Avars," comprising all modern France, half of modern Germany, four-fifths of modern Italy, and all of modern Switzerland.

Restoration of the Empire in the West (A. D. 800).— By the invitation of Pope Leo X. Charlemagne made a third visit to Rome in the year 800. On Christmas Day "the king came into the basilica of the blessed St. Peter, to attend the celebration of mass. At the moment when in his place before the altar he was bowing down to pray, Pope Leo placed upon his head a golden crown, and all the Roman people shouted, 'Long life and victory to Charles Augustus, crowned by God the great and pacific emperor of the Romans!'"—*L. H. Farmer.*

The empire in the west was thus revived and Charlemagne was the successor of the Cæsars of Rome, emperor of France, of Germany, and of Italy.

Renown of Charlemagne.—Charlemagne's title to the imperial crown was recognized, though with reluctance, by the emperor of the East. His renown spread into Asia. "Haroun-al-Raschid, the Arabian caliph at Bagdad, being an enemy of the Moors in Spain, sent gifts to the great king of the Franks—an elephant, a beautiful tent, a set of costly chessmen, and a water-clock, so arranged that every hour a little brazen ball fell into a brass basin, and little figures of knights, from one to twelve according to the hour, came out and paraded about in front."—*Miss Yonge's "Young Folks' History of Germany."*

Schools.—But it was not only as a great warrior that Charlemagne is famous. He improved the laws and encouraged agriculture, established schools, founding at Paris the first university of Europe. "He gathered round him in his palace at Aix-la-Chapelle men of education from all nations, and, first of all modern monarchs, he encouraged learning."

"In his palace he established a school, with great scholars at its head, and there, with as many noblemen's sons and other young men as chose to attend, he studied astronomy, theology, law, grammar, rhetoric, and music."

Discussions on philosophy were held, and the monk Alcuin explained the theories of Pythagoras, Aristotle and Plato, or quoted Homer, Virgil, and Pliny. In their enthusiasm they took the names of their classical favorites, the king himself representing the royal Hebrew, David. Charlemagne was so fond of study that he had books read to him at meals and often stinted his sleep to gain time. "He learned Latin and Greek, and improved his native German by inventing German words for the months and the winds." He paid great attention to astronomy, could calculate the courses of planets in his head. He caused a German grammar to be commenced, an attempt which was not repeated for hundreds of years. But with all his learning there was one thing he could not accomplish, which was to write a good hand. Though he kept his tablets under his pillow that he might improve any odd moments day or night, the hand that could so easily wield the ponderous iron lance was conquered by the pen.—*Adapted*.

Government.—His government was a model for those times. His subjects so diverse in nationality and education were held under a most wise and powerful authority. The monarchy which he founded was strong in himself alone and when he died it perished with him. Yet each piece of his great empire possessed enough of the vitalizing force which his mind and wisdom had given it to enable it to rise an empire by itself. So, though Charlemagne's kingdom could not be preserved by his successors, from that great power rose the separate empires of France, Germany, and Italy.—*Adapted*.

Death of Charlemagne.—"Charlemagne died in 814, in his seventy-first year, and was buried at Aix-la-Chapelle sitting upright, robed and crowned, in his chair with a sword by his side."—*Miss Yonge*.

"There is a beautiful legend that Charlemagne visits the Rhine yearly and blesses the vintage. He comes in a golden robe, and crosses the river on a golden bridge, and the bells of heaven chime above him as he fulfills his peaceful mission. The fine superstition is celebrated in music and verse."—*Butterworth's "Zigzag Journey of Northern Lands."* Learn "Die Wacht am Rhein."

LEGEND OF CHARLEMAGNE.

By the Rhine, the emerald river,
  How softly flows the night!
The vine-clad hills are lying
  In the moonbeam's golden light.

And on the hillside walketh
  A kingly shadow down,
With sword and purple mantle,
  And heavy golden crown.

'Tis Charlemagne, the emperor,
  Who, with a powerful hand,
For many a hundred years
  Hath ruled in German land.

From out his grave in Aachen
  He hath arisen there,
To bless once more his vineyards,
  And breath their fragrant air.

By Rudesheim, on the water,
  The moon doth brightly shine,
And buildeth a bridge of gold
  Across the emerald Rhine.

The emperor walketh over,
  And all along the tide
Bestows his benediction
  On the vineyard far and wide.

"Then turns he back to Aachen
  In his grave-sleep to remain,
Till the New Year's fragrant clusters
  Shall call him forth again.
    —*Emanuel Geibel.* From "Zigzag Journey."

Division of Charlemagne's Empire.—The mighty empire of Charlemagne, which was at first bestowed upon his son Louis, soon fell to pieces like the kingdom of Alexander. The grandsons, Louis, Charles, and Lothaire, quarreled over their respective shares, and after the dreadful "Battle of the Brothers," a treaty was made which divided the empire among them (843).

East Frankland or Germany was given to Louis. West Frankland or France to Charles, and the middle portions of the Frankish territory, including Italy and a long strip extending to the North Sea, between the dominions of his brothers, was given to Lothaire. This strip of land later took the name of Lotharingia or Lorraine.

From the time of this treaty in 843 the separation between France and Germany was fairly accomplished. At that time the two countries spoke different languages though the French king clung for awhile to his Teutonic dress and manners. In 1843 Germany celebrated its 1000th anniversary.

RISE OF MODERN NATIONS.

I. ENGLAND.

Anglo-Saxon Conquest.—(See "Roman Conquest" in Roman History.) About the time Alaric and the Visigoths appeared before the gates of Rome (A. D. 410), the legions were recalled from England and the frontier of the Rhine and the Danube, to protect the provinces nearer Italy. "This was a signal for the Picts and Scots to renew their incursions; and the Britons in their need are said to have solicited the aid of the Saxons, a German tribe near the Elbe. (Read Saxon Boy in "Ten Boys.")

"These Saxons together with their neighbors the Angles were powerful sea-rulers on the German Ocean and Baltic Sea. They delighted in storms and tempests, and in their small vessels of osiers, covered with skins, they courageously sailed amidst the rough winds and foaming surges of the German Ocean, in search of conquest and wild adventure. They were clothed in loose and flowing garments, and wore their hair long, floating about their shoulders."—*L. H. Farmer.*

Under the leadership of Hengist and Horsa these Saxons landed on the island of Thanet, at the mouth of the Thames, about the year 449. Vortigern, the king of Britain, offered to give them a large tract of country in the part of the country where they had landed, if they would aid him in his contest with his enemies. Hengist and Horsa agreed to this proposal and they soon succeeded in defeating the Picts and Scots and driving them back to their mountains in the north. They received as recompense the island of Thanet, and it is related that Hengist gave his daughter Rowena in marriage to Vortigern to strengthen the alliance more closely. In six years' time Hengist took possession of the country between the Thames and the English channel, making Canterbury his capital. From that time it was the ambition of all the chiefs of the Saxon pirates to gain a firm footing in Great Britain, as the Frankish tribes had done in Gaul. "At last the Britons became alarmed at the increasing power of the Anglo-Saxons, and the result was a fierce contest. It is related that King Vortigern, with three hundred of his officers, were invited by Hengist to a feast, and a quarrel having arisen, an affray occurred, in which the Britons were all killed, except Vortigern, who was taken prisoner, and was only ransomed by ceding three whole provinces to his captors.

"The famous King Arthur, whose Knights of the Round Table have been so celebrated in fable and song, was a king of the Britons during these wars between his people and the Saxons."—*L. H. Farmer*. He defeated them, it is said, in twelve battles, killing with his own hand in a single day 400 of his enemies. "When wounded, he was borne to an island formed by two rivers and died there, at what date is not known. His tomb has never been found. The Cambrians, whom he had defended so long, refused to believe in the death of their national hero, and for many centuries looked forward to his coming as the time of their deliverance. (See Tennyson's "King Arthur," also prose stories of "King Arthur and the Knights of the Round Table.")

In two hundred years after this the Saxon power became supreme and the remaining Britons sought refuge in Wales, Cornwall, and Brittany. The Saxons founded seven states in England, each one having a separate ruler; but, after a series of wars with each other, they were united in 827, under Egbert, who thus became sole monarch of England (Angle-land).

"The Saxons were converted to Christianity at the close of the sixth century. Pope Gregory the Great, when a young deacon, passing through the Roman market place, observed some fair-haired youths exposed for sale as slaves. Struck by their beauty he inquired to what country they belonged. Being informed that they were Angles, he exclaimed, 'Not Angles, but angels.'" —*Quackenbos*. In after days he remembered the fair captives, and sent Au'gustine at the head of an embassy to Ethelbert, king of Kent, with a view to the conversion of their people. When the entreaties of his Christian queen, who was the daughter of a Frankish king, were united to the eloquence of Augustine, Ethelbert yielded, was baptized, and Christianity soon became the established faith of Saxon England

Danish Invasion.—During the reign of Egbert, the first Saxon king, England, like France and Germany, was ravaged by hordes of northern pirates. "These sea-rovers came from Norway, Sweden, and Denmark, and in search of plunder sailed the stormiest seas fearlessly in open boats without decks. They were as valiant fighters as they were expert mariners. They would land near a sea-coast town, rob it of everything that was worth taking, and escape with their booty." Those who invaded England were called Danes, though they were not exclusively the natives of Denmark, but came from all the shores of the Northern and Baltic seas. They were successfully repelled by Egbert's grandson, Alfred the Great.

(Adapted from Bonner's "Child's History of France" and L. H. Farmer's "Boys' Book of Famous Rulers.")

Alfred the Great.—In the year 871, Alfred the Great, one of the best and wisest kings that ever ruled England, succeeded to the throne when he was twenty-two years of age.

"Twice in his childhood he had been taken to Rome, where the Saxon nobles were in the habit of going on journeys which they supposed to be religious; and once he had staid for some time in Paris. Learning, however, was so little cared for, then, that at twelve years old he had not been taught to read." "His mother, one day, showed him and his brothers a book of Saxon poetry, which was beautifully written and ornamented, and told them that she would give it to the one who should soonest learn to peruse it. Alfred applied himself with so much ardor, that in a very short time he was able to read the poem to the queen, who gave it to him as his reward. From this time he took the greatest delight in study; but he had two great difficulties to struggle with; one was, that there were so few books to be had; and the other, that there were so few people among the Saxons who could teach him anything.

"Notwithstanding all these obstacles, he soon became one of the most learned men of his time. Even when he was king, he always carried a book in the bosom of his robe, that, whenever he had a spare moment, he might be able to profit by it; and thus, without neglecting any of his duties, he acquired a very extensive knowledge.

"His time was divided into three equal parts; one-third was devoted to study, another third to sleep and refreshment, and the other to the affairs of his kingdom. As there were no clocks or watches in use in England, Alfred contrived to measure time by the burning of candles. They were painted in rings of different breadths and colors—so many colors as he had duties to attend to, and thus he knew by the burning of these candles when he had been employed long enough about any one thing. But he found that when the wind blew upon them, they burnt more quickly; and so, to remedy the inconvenience, he invented lanterns.

"During the first eight years of his reign, he suffered continual persecution from the Danes, who at last obtained almost entire possession of the kingdom, and Alfred was obliged to conceal himself.

"At one time he assumed the disguise of a servant and hired himself to a cow-herd. One day, when he was in the cottage trimming his bow and arrows, the old man's wife, who did not know that he was king, told him to watch some cakes that were baking by the fire. Alfred; who had many other things to think of, forgot to turn them at the proper time, and they were spoiled. The old woman was very angry with him, and told him he was a lazy fellow, who would eat the cakes, though he would not take the trouble to turn them.

"Resolving to learn by personal observation the exact strength of the enemy, he disguised himself as a harper, and entered the Danish camp. When Guthrum, the general of the Danes, heard him play and sing he was so much pleased with him, that he made him stay for some days in the camp, supposing him to be some poor minstrel.

"Alfred made good use of his eyes all this time. He observed that the Danes, not thinking that the English could muster another army strong enough to attack them, were quite off their guard, and were dancing and singing, and thought of nothing but amusing themselves.

"The king, having gained all the knowledge he wanted, slipped out of the camp, and throwing off his disguises, summoned his faithful subjects to meet him near Salwood Forest. The English, who had believed their beloved monarch to be dead, received the summons with great gladness, and joyfully resorted to the appointed place.

"Alfred did not allow their ardor to cool, but led them against the enemy, who were completely defeated. Instead of killing or making slaves of the prisoners, as was often done in that barbarous age, he permitted them, upon their becoming Christians and promising to live honestly, to remain in England.

"They established themselves in East Anglia and Northumberland; but they and their descendants proved very troublesome subjects.

"After the victory over Guthrum, England enjoyed many years of peace and tranquility. These were devoted by Alfred to repairing the mischief which had been done by the Danes. The churches and monasteries, as they contained the greatest riches, so they had been the first objects of attack and destruction.

"To repair these might seem no very difficult matter, for most of them were built of wood, and covered with thatch. Stones were only used in building castles and strong places of defense. When the Saxons came into Britain, they found a great many beautiful palaces, baths, churches, and other buildings of stone, which had been erected by the Romans. Some of them were built with so much solidity that they would have remained to this day, if they had not been willfully destroyed. This was done by the Saxons, who made it a rule to destroy every town or castle that they took, instead of preserving them for their own use. They had been accustomed to live in wretched hovels, made of earth or wood, and covered with straw or the branches of trees; nor did they much improve their knowledge of architecture for two hundred years after their arrival in Britain.

"Toward the close of the seventh century, two Saxon clergymen, who were great travelers and had acquired some taste for architecture during their frequent visits to Rome, resolved to attempt an improvement in the the taste of their Saxon countrymen. They brought to England a number of masons, in order to build the church of their monastery of stone, after the Roman manner. "When the work was far advanced, agents were sent into France to procure glassmakers. These not only performed the work required of them, but taught the Saxons the art of making glass for windows, lamps, drinking-vessels, and other uses. The ancient Britons, indeed, were acquainted with this art, but the Saxons had never before acquired it.

"This stone building with glass windows was an object of great curiosity and admiration, but did not find many imitators. When Alfred resolved to rebuild his ruined churches and monasteries, and to adorn his cities with stone buildings, he was obliged to send to foreign countries for workmen. But even in King Alfred's time the use of stone did not become general, and glass windows were only to be seen in churches.

"When the Romans invaded England, they instructed and improved those whom they subdued. But darkness and desolation marked the course of the fierce and illiterate Saxons.

"As you may well suppose, Alfred was a liberal encourager of learning. He established many schools and founded the University at Oxford. There were many impediments to progress in learning in those days. Books were very scarce and dear, so that few but kings and rich monasteries could afford to buy them. Alfred gave a great estate in land for a single volume on geography.

"Paper was not yet invented, and parchment enough could not be had for a great supply of books." Neither was printing invented for a long time afterward. There were no signs to represent numbers except the Roman letters I. V. C. C. M. The study of arithmetic was pronounced by Aldehelm, a learned Saxon bishop, to be almost too difficult for the mind of man. It was made easier by the use of the figures 1, 2, 3, 4, etc., which were used by the Arabians and introduced into England about the year 1130.

"Alfred also endeavored to improve his subjects in the useful and ingenius arts, and invited many skillful foreign workmen to instruct them. The English goldsmiths soon became very expert." "But the workmen most highly regarded were the blacksmiths, because they could make swords and other instruments of war. Every soldier of rank was constantly attended by his smith to keep his arms in order. The chief smith was an officer of great dignity at court. At table he sat next to the priest, and was entitled to a draught of every kind of liquor brought into the hall.

"Alfred was very desirous of creating a strong naval force, considering that to be the surest defense against the Danes. But he had great difficulties to struggle with. His subjects knew nothing of ship-building, so he was obliged to get foreign ship-builders. In time his own subjects learned how to build ships, but there was a new difficulty—he had no sailors. These were also procured from other countries, and at last a considerable fleet was constructed. This fleet did not prove a very effectual defense, for the Danes, coming in 330 vessels, under a famous leader named Hastings, succeeded in landing at Kent. A long contest ensued. At length the wife and children of Hastings were taken prisoners. Alfred gave them back on condition that all the Danes should leave the country.

"The remainder of the reign of this truly great king was prosperous. He lived beloved by his subjects, feared by his enemies, and admired by all mankind. The English, and, as their descendants, we, are indebted to the wisdom of Alfred for many very useful laws and valuable rights. Among the rest, he instituted the right of trial by jury. Something like this had existed among the Saxons from the earliest times, but Alfred first reduced it to a regular system and secured it by positive laws.

"Alfred died in 901 in the forty-ninth year of his age."—*S. G. Goodrich.*

II. FRANCE.

The Norsemen Invade France.—Even before the death of Charlemagne France had suffered by the depredations of the Norsemen or Northmen. That great monarch is said to have wept at the thought of the calamities which would befall his country after his death. He explained the cause of his tears to his courtiers, saying, "I fear not these pirates during my lifetime, but I foresee what evils they will heap upon my descendants and people."

"Every year, as soon as the spring-birds began to sing, these sea-rovers came swooping down upon the coasts of France landing in some sheltered cove, seizing money, jewels, food, cattle, and slaves, and dashing off to sea again with their booty. By and by they were not content with the sea-coast. They sailed up the rivers in their broad boats, fashioned in the shape of a serpent or a bird of prey, ribbed with iron, and provided with great beaks of bronze and ivory. Back of this beak stood a warrior, shouting, singing, gesticulating, to strike terror into the hearts of those who saw him."—*Bonner.*

A branch of these same Northmen, whose chiefs were called Vikings, found their way across the northern ocean to Iceland and Greenland, and it is supposed they landed in New England five hundred years before Columbus discovered America, but as they did not find anything worth stealing they went away. They found their way across the ocean by letting loose a hawk and following his flight, each ship being provided with a cage of these birds.

"When the poor French peasants saw a fleet of these boats come round the hill, dashing the foam from their bows, and heard the horn and war cries of the warriors on the beach, they fled as swiftly as they could, with wives and children, and, if they had time, with such of their belongings as they could snatch up, to the nearest castle or monastery. Sometimes the count or the abbot was strong enough to give battle to the pirates. Convents, churches, and castles were generally robbed and their owners killed under their own roofs."—*Bonner.* The only way to induce the Northmen to leave the country was to bribe them. In the reign of Charles, the grandson of Charlemagne, they sailed up the Seine, and departed only on the payment of several thousand pounds of silver. This tribute was demanded year after year, until finally in 911 Charles the Simple gave them the northern part of France, on condition that they would leave the rest in peace and embrace Christianity. The territory thus ceded was called from them Normandy, and the name Northmen became softened into Normans.

"Their valiant chief Rollo was so tall that he could not find a horse in Norway large enough for him to ride, and going on his expeditions afoot, he was called Rollo the Marcher."—*Quackenbos.* When told that for the valuable grant of land he must do homage to the King of France he delegated the ceremony to one of his followers. This ceremony consisted of kneeling before the king or over-lord, at the same time swearing to follow him in war and be henceforth his man (Latin *homo*, whence "homage.") "The over-lord, in his turn, swore to aid him and be a true good lord to him in return, and kissed his brow. In return the under-lord, or vassal as he was called, was to kiss the foot of his superior. This was paying homage. Kings thus paid homage and swore allegiance to the emperor; dukes or counts to kings; lesser counts or barons to dukes; and for the lands they owned they were bound to serve their lord in council and in war, and not to fight against him. Lands so held were called fiefs, and the whole was called the feudal system. Now, Rollo was to hold his lands in fief from the king, and he swore his oath, but he was too proud to stoop to kiss the foot of King Charles. The Northman he chose to perform the ceremony was as proud as himself, and instead of kneeling, lifted the king's foot to his lips, so that poor Charles the Simple was upset, throne and all."—*Miss Yonge.*

"Rollo was thus made a peer of France and received the title of Duke. He became a sincere Christian. Under his government, the churches were rebuilt, the fields were cultivated and robbery was almost unknown." In a short time these barbarians had adopted the language, manners, and religion of the French, and Normandy under their rule became the fairest province of France. The heathen Vikings, delighting in the wild life of sea-rover and pirate, had been transformed into Christian knights, eager for pilgrimages and crusades. (Read Norman Boy in "Ten Boys.")

Feudalism.—During the terror of the invasion of the Norsemen the people naturally turned for protection to the neighboring lords, whose castles were their only refuge. The kings were powerless to defend or govern. The peasant was the one who suffered the most. In the north of France, bands of Northmen, in the south, bands of Moors, in the southeast, bands of Hungarians, whose faces had been slashed to make them look more hideous, marched into the country at harvest time and carried off the ripe crops. To resist the robbers, the peasants armed themselves and selected one of their bravest men to lead them. In order to distinguish him from the rest he received the name of lord, or seigneur, duke, count or baron. It was agreed that the land should belong to the lord and the peasant should hold it on lease from him. As there was very little money at that time in the country parts of France, the rent consisted of a quart of grain, a pig, or a fat goose once a year for a field or an acre. It was also agreed that whenever the lord called upon the tenants to go forth to battle they were bound to do so.

This was the feudal system, which, though it was greatly abused in later years, was the only protection for life and property at the time it was invented. The land which was owned by the feudal lords and leased to their tenants was called a "fief," and the tenants were called "vassals."

Originally this relation of vassalage had nothing to do with the possession of land, but was a position of especial honor. As the custom of rewarding service with gifts of land became fixed, it was natural that the vassals should be first rewarded. Instead of keeping a standing army the Frankish kings found it far more convenient to give their lands into the hands of faithful subjects who should hold them and cultivate them and in return should not only agree to serve them in person, but to furnish upon their call a certain number of armed men ready and equipped for active military service. In like manner the vassals of the king granted estates to their followers, who were called their vassals, and attended them in battle. This array of lords, with their retainers, constituted the feudal army.—*Adapted*.

The castles in which the nobles or lords lived were enormous buildings, either round or square, massive, without ornament, and generally built on hills. "They were pierced with a few loop-holes, from which arrows could be shot, and had a single gate opening on a moat which could only be crossed by a draw-bridge; they were crowned with battlements from which masses of rock, pitch, and melted lead were thrown upon an assailant who had been bold enough to approach the foot of the wall. The castles, the ruin of which are seen along the Rhine and in Scotland and France, now look like gray, jagged, and broken crows' nests torn by storms. Those who had no right to live inside the castle itself, who were neither nobles nor warriors, established themselves at the foot of the great walls, under their mighty guardianship. In this way many European cities were formed. Those who built the castle, made the clothing and armor of the knights and baked the bread were called 'serfs.' One step higher than these were the free tenants called 'villeins.' Unlike the serfs, they had their liberty, and, on condition of a yearly rent, they held the lands which they were able to transmit to their children."—*Duruy and Emerton*. (Read Lowell's "Sir Launfal.")

"In the course of time these feudal lords came to be kings in fact, if not in name, in their respective fiefs. They had their own armies, their own courts, their own mints, their own system of taxes, their own laws, quite independent of the king at Paris. They were, it is true, required to pay homage to the king, which consisted in holding his stirrup when he was riding, or some such idle formality; but practically the king had no authority over them at all. The peasants knew no superior but their own feudal lord."—*Bonner*.

The kingdom of *Hugh Capet*, who had been chosen by the bishops and nobles in 987 as the *first king of all France*, was cut down to only a small territory along the Seine and Loire. Indeed he was only king in name, for Normandy, Burgundy, Aquitaine, Campagne, Toulouse, each had its separate government. The Duke of Aquitaine, who was a feudal lord, ruled a much larger country, and so did the Duke of Burgundy.

The king and the church were constantly jealous of the power of the nobles, but in their grim strongholds they continued to defy all authority until the close of the Middle Ages. The Crusades first broke the strength of feudalism and the introduction of fire-arms completed its downfall. (See page 426, Myers.)

Chivalry.—In the days of Hugh Capet, there was very little good in the world. All France was in a turbulent, cruel, and savage state. It was the belief of all good Christians that the world was to come to an end, and that the Day of Judgment was to come in the year 1000. The fields were left untilled, and in consequence, famines and epidemic diseases broke out. "In the midst of these dark days some French nobles, filled with pity for the wretchedness they saw around them, united to remedy existing evils. They pledged themselves to defend the weak and become the champions of the oppressed; the church blessed their undertaking;" and thus the institution of *Chivalry* was established, the germs of which were found in society before the age of Charlemagne. The name of Chivalry was applied to the system, from the *chevaliers* who enrolled themselves in its support and who constituted the order of knighthood, to which admission was obtained by formal ceremony. From France this institution rapidly spread to England, Spain, Germany, and Italy, in all of which countries the Teutonic race was now established.—*Adapted*.

All persons of gentle blood, except those designed for the church, followed the profession of arms and were trained from childhood in the duties and exercises of knighthood. In early youth they lived as pages in the courts of the nobles or of the king. There in the presence of high-born ladies and knights, they were trained to serve their mistress and imitate the gallantry of their superiors. Their studies were limited to music, chess, and memorizing their Latin Code of Manners. They were intrusted with the messages of the lady of the castle, cared for her falcon, and obeyed her slightest wish. "In the tender days of his pagehood he first learned the lesson of love and reverence, cherishing, as of inestimable value, the slight favor from his lady's hand. The depth of this feeling is illustrated in a German romance, which represents a devoted page as opening a wound in his bosom to lay gold thread which his mistress had given him, as near as possible to his heart. His lady's presence was the greatest incentive to valorous deeds that a knight could have. He wore her scarf, ribbon, or glove on his helmet, and in her name would make the most extravagant vows and swear to perform impossible feats. And sometimes her caprice would exact from him achievements which taxed both strength and courage to the utmost. We read that at a German court some knights and ladies were viewing two lions confined in an inclosure, when one of the ladies threw in her glove and commanded her lover to recover it. He leaped in, threw his mantle over the beasts as they rushed toward him, picked up the glove and sprung out in safety; but even his loyalty could not blind him to his lady's unreasonable caprice, and he immediately renounced one who could wantonly subject her true knight to such danger."—*Quackenbos.*

"At the age of fourteen the page was made a squire and his training became more severe. He was taught to endure fatique, thirst, and hunger, to run long distances, to turn somersaults in heavy armor, to wield his weapons with agility and skill, and to manage his fiery barb with grace and dexterity."—*Quackenbos.* He was also assigned to duties about the castle such as setting and serving a table, grooming the horses, or caring for the armor of the knights. Each squire served some individual knight whom he was bound to obey, to attend in battle, and serve with his very life in case of need.

"Although he attends his lord in battle, he is not expected to take part in the fight. He is in little danger, for, as he wears no armor, it is considered dishonorable for a knight to attack him. He stands ready to render any assistance which his lord may require. If he is overthrown, he helps him to rise; if he is wounded, he carries him from the field; if the wound is mortal, he receives his lord's dying commands, and, after his death, bestows upon his body an honorable burial.

"An early English writer thus describes the exercises of the youth: 'Crowds of noble and sprightly youths, mounted on war horses, admirably trained to perform all their turnings and evolutions, ride into the fields in distinct bands, armed with lances and shields, and exhibit representations of battles. The hope of victory rouses the spirits of these noble youths. Their fiery horses neigh and prance, and champ their foaming bits. At length the signal is given and the sports begin. The youths, divided into opposite bands, encounter one another. In one place some flee and others pursue, without overtaking them. In another place, one of the bands overtakes and overturns the other.'"

At the age of twenty-one, the young noble's probation is over. "If he is perfect in his martial exercises, courteous in his demeanor, polite and attentive to the ladies, obedient to his superiors, respectful to his elders, skilled in music and dancing, possessed, in short, of all knightly accomplishments, he is admitted to the order of knights. The candidate for knighthood prepares himself by fasting and praying. Having bathed and clothed himself in a white garment, as a symbol of the purity and truth that must distinguish his future life, he enters the church, and, advancing to the altar, presents his sword to the priest, who blesses it and then returns it to him. The novice then, with clasped hands, falls upon his knees before the elder knight, who takes from him the sword, and administers the oath. He swears to speak the truth; to maintain the right; to protect the distressed; to practice courtesy; to defend his religion; to despise the allurements of ease, and to vindicate in every perilous adventure the honor of his name. He is then invested by the knights, or ladies, or damsels present, with the exterior marks of chivalry—his spurs, his coat of mail, his brassards (the covering for the arms), his gauntlets or iron gloves, and, lastly, his sword is buckled on. Then the elder knight, rising from his seat, gives him the blow on his shoulders with the flat of the sword, saying: 'In the name of God, of St. George, and of St. Michael the Archangel, I make thee knight, rise up, Sir John!' or 'Sir Thomas,' or whatever his name may be. The helmet, buckler, and lance are now given, after which, mounting, and curvetting his steed, brandishing his lance, and glittering his sword, the new knight parades about amidst the acclamations of the people.

"Sometimes an esquire had an opportunity of performing some gallant action in battle, and was knighted upon the field. This was esteemed the most honorable mode of obtaining it. Such knights were called knights-bannerets. Others devoted their lives to the protection of the injured and helpless. They were not formed into any regular body, but were quite independent of one another, and traveled about from place to place for the purpose of redressing grievances. These were called knights-errant. This class of knights might well do a great amount of good in those lawless times, when might made right. The whole institution of chivalry did infinite service in softening the ferocious manners of the times."—*S. G. Goodrich.* (Condition of the Family in

Feudal Times—Duruy. page 214. Read Sir Walter Scott's "Ivanhoe.")

ENGLAND IN THE MIDDLE AGES—*Continued*.

Danish Conquest.—England continued to prosper during the rule of the son of Alfred the Great and his grandson, Athelstan. In the eleventh century the sovereigns were men of feeble minds and the Anglo-Saxons became a submissive, unwarlike people. During the reign of Ethelred the Unready, the Danes grew more powerful. After several times purchasing peace from the invaders, Ethelred secretly ordered a massacre of all the Danes in the country (1002). As might have been expected the Danes retaliated by sweeping like a whirlwind through distracted England. Finally the king of Denmark himself came with a great fleet. " The beaks of the ships were of brass and under the beaks were figure-heads, finely carved and painted, of men and bulls and dolphins. On the mast-heads were figures of birds and dragons to serve for weathercocks, and the sterns were adorned with golden lions." (Church's "Stories of England.")

The English were powerless to resist him and Ethelred fled over the sea to France. The sudden death of the King of Denmark prevented the Danes from gaining the immediate possession of the island, but in 1016, his son, *Canute*, became king of Engand. He was also ruler of Denmark, Norway, and Sweden. His wise and impartial rule did much to conciliate the English and for eighteen years England prospered under Danish rule. "His regard for the laws is shown by the following anecdote: Having in a moment of anger slain a soldier, he insisted on being tried and sentenced like any common offender. His judges decided that he should inflict his own penalty, and, as murder was then punished by a fine, he paid 360 talents.

"Another anecdote is told of the method which he used to rebuke his flattering courtiers. They carried their absurd adulation to so extravagant a length as to declare in his presence that the very elements were under his control, and nothing in nature dared disobey his commands.

"One day while walking with his attendants by the seaside at Southampton he undertook to rebuke this servile flattery in a striking manner. He ordered his chair to be placed on the beach while the tide was beginning to rise, and taking his seat he exclaimed to the waters in a voice of authority, 'O Sea! Thou art under my control, and the land on which I sit is mine. I charge thee to approach no further, nor dare to wet the feet of thy sovereign!' But the rising billows, regardless of his command, dashed upon the shore and forced him to retire. The king turned to his flatterers and said: 'Learn from this example the insignificance of all human power, and that God alone is omnipotent!' He then took the crown from his head and, we are told, never wore it afterwards, but ordered it to be put on the image of the crucified Christ."—*Goodrich.*

"Amid the cares of his extensive kingdom, Canute found time for pious works, built churches, and went on a pilgrimage to Rome."—*Quackenbos.*

"After his death in 1036, his sons, *Harold*, *Harefoot* and *Hardicanute*, successively held the crown." The sons lacked their father's ability and contests arose which in seven years resulted in the restoration of the old Saxon line.

Edward the Confessor, the son of Ethelred, ascended the throne in 1042 and was hailed with joy by the people. Their joy, however, was of short duration, for having spent part of his life in Normandy, he introduced the language and customs of that country, and filled the court with Norman favorites. This provoked a rebellion on the part of the Saxon nobles, and in the end the odious foreigners were outlawed. Edward was devout in his ways, though a negligent ruler, and for this reason gained the surname of Confessor. He is said to have spent a tenth part of the whole wealth of the kingdom in building a great church at *Westminster*, the precursor of the magnificent church built afterwards by King Henry III. Edward was too ill to be present at the consecration, December 28, 1065, and died a few days after. He was buried in his new church where his tomb may be seen at the present day.

Harold, a prominent Saxon noble, was chosen king of England and was crowned at Westminster. "He did not find the throne a peaceable possession; for *William, Duke of Normandy*, immediately asserted his right to it, under pretense that Edward had left him the kingdom in his will. To maintain his claim, William went with a large army to England, where he landed on the 28th of September, 1066.—*Adapted*.

Norman Conquest of England.—"On the 14th of October, 1066, was fought the great battle of Hastings, a battle that completely changed the fate of England. Harold was killed by a wound in the eye with an arrow, and William gained a complete victory. The result of this conflict threw the English into the utmost consternation.

"Some of the nobles assembled at London to deliberate in regard to the successor to the throne, but before they had time to come to a decision William, *the Conqueror*, was at the gates. The greater part of the nobles went to meet him and offered him the vacant throne, which he, with a little pretended hesitation, accepted. He was crowned at Westminster on Christmas Day, 1066, and thus was completed the *Conquest of England*, as it is called."—*S. G. Goodrich.*

"William began his reign with so much prudence and moderation that his new subjects thought they had great reason to be satisfied. But whilst he treated them with seeming confidence and friendship, he took care to place all real power in the hands of the Normans. He everywhere disarmed the Saxons and built fortresses in all the principal cities, placing Norman soldiers in them."—*Goodrich.*

"The Anglo-Saxons, however, were not entirely subdued; they broke out into insurrections, and at last the king, determining to strike terror into their hearts, marched northward, burned their towns, and put thousands to the sword."—*Quackenbos.*

"The Anglo-Saxon nobility were driven into exile, or dispossessed of their territories, and the greater part of all the landed property of England fell into the hands of the king, who rewarded his followers for their services by granting them the domains which he had seized or confiscated. He made military service the indispensable condition of these donations, and thus England was soon covered with strong castles, and the feudal system became established to the full extent." The Normans called themselves after their castles and fortified towns, thus introducing *surnames.—Peter Parley*.

Formation of English Language.—As a part of his plan for reducing the Anglo-Saxon to complete subjection William used every means to introduce the Norman-French language and manners into England and to eradicate that of the Anglo-Saxon. "French was taught in the schools, spoken at court and employed exclusively in the tribunals of law. He could not, however, compel its use by the lower classes. They obstinately adhered to their own vernacular; and not till their prejudices against their conquerors had been softened by the lapse of fifty years were they willing to modify their own tongue and enlarge its vocabulary by drawing on the language of the Normans. From this time changes were rapidly made; and the grafting of numerous elements from the versatile Norman-French upon the homely but nervous Saxon stock produced our present English (about 1350)."—*Quackenbos*. (See "Ivanhoe," by Sir Walter Scott.)

"Among the oppressive institutions of this monarch were the Forest Laws and the Curfew. William was especially fond of hunting, and not content with sixty-eight deer friths, besides parks and chases, he made what was called the New Forest, by laying waste a tract of thirty square miles, demolishing churches, and destroying hundreds of homes. The Curfew was a bell rung at eight o'clock as a signal for extinguishing lights and fires." "Its original design is said to have been to prevent nightly meetings for conspirators."—*Quackenbos and Peter Parley.*

Benefits Derived from Norman Conquest.—The Norman Conquest, strange as it may seem, left many of the civil institutions of the Saxons undestroyed, or changed only in name. The Wittenagemote (see Miss Andrew's "Ten Boys") still survived under the appellation of *parliament*. The liberties of England were not abridged. On the countrary it established a powerful and active aristocracy, which was strong enough at times to give the law to the sovereign. It promoted the emancipation of the slaves and protected the privileges of the free.

"The greatest benefit derived by England from the Norman conquest was the new vigor and spirit which it gave to the national mind." A new race of men, inspired by that love of glory which made every Norman restless till he had acquired personal improvement and distinction, was spread over the kingdom. "The wealth and situation of England opened new avenues to fame, and drew from all parts of Europe the most aspiring and the most able men to enter the lists for honor and profit. A new creative vigor appeared afterward in every field of human merit. Activity and enterprise became the characteristic qualities of the nation; and the different classes, attaching themselves to various pursuits, infused the spirits and enlarged the boundaries of improvement in all. In war, in religion, literature, trade, and amusements, the Anglo-Normans became active and indefatigable." (From Peter Parley's "European History.")

Literature and Arts.—"During the reign of William the Conqueror's son, Henry I, the manufacture of cloth first received attention in England. Paper made from rags became common, and parchment went out of use. Agriculture was greatly improved by the Normans; the land was drained, and the wastes produced by the Danish wars were restored to fertility."

The stories of "King Arthur and the Knights of the Round Table" were published for the first time, also a reliable History of England. "Poetry, music, and architecture were diligently cultivated. Abbeys and churches were erected on all sides, and adorned with paintings and statues. Monks were the principal architects and builders of these edifices. The monks also constructed organs, the chief, if not the only instrument used in worship, and spent much time in illuminating manuscripts, an art that now attained great perfection."—*Quackenbos.*

III. GERMANY.

Comparison with France.—In Germany, also, feudalism took deep root during the terrible Norseman invasions. Germany contained five separate nations—Franks, Saxons, Thuringians, Bavarians, and Swabians—whose dukes were almost independent in their realms. In France the crown gradually absorbed the feudal states, and so formed a powerful kingdom; but in Germany the power of the crown, though strong at first, became weak. The royal family dying out in the second or third generation, made it necessary that the ancient system of election should be restored in Germany at the very time when it disappeared from the customs of France. The struggle between the king and the feudal lords was alike in both countries—but the results were different. Germany had no central city for capital like Paris, around which the national sentiment could grow, and while France reached an extreme centralization, Germany become more and more divided.

Ancient People of Austria.—At this period Germany was continually ravaged by the Magyars or Hungarians, who had left their original abodes in the Ural mountains and were occupying the plains of Hungary. These barbarians were even more cruel than the Norsemen; they were believed to be cannibals, and to drink the blood of their enemies.

In 918, *Henry, the Duke of Saxony*, was chosen king because he was thought to be the only man who had skill enough to defend Germany against the barbarians. Though victorious in his first battle with them, he was forced to make a truce for nine years, and pay them a tribute in gold. This time he spent in training his people in arms. He instituted games that are said to have been the beginning of the tournament. All men of lower rank were to be trained in arms from their thirteenth year, and were commanded to meet near the villages every three days to drill. Seeing the need of walled cities, he ordained that every ninth man of the district should be stationed in the nearest "burg," or fortress, while the others were to keep his fields in cultivation. This was the origin of the *burghers* of Germany.

"He built also storehouses in the fortresses in which one-third of all the crops were to be deposited, and he required that their assemblies and markets, their public festivals and marriages, should be held within the walls."

When his country was well prepared for a war Henry defied the Hungarians and totally defeated them, driving them back into their country. Shortly after their second defeat by Henry's successor, they embraced Christianity, and under Stephen the Pius (1,000) advanced in the arts of peace. The military province established by the Germans between their country and Germany was at first called Oster (East) March, a name since changed to Austria.—*Adapted from Duruy, Miss Yonge, and Barnes.*

Otto the Great, the son of Henry, was crowned king at Aix-la-Chapelle a short time before his father's death. "The dukes, princes, and all the great noblemen of the country assembled in the 'Hall of Columns,' where stood the throne of Charlemagne, and proclaimed him king. After his election the archbishop of Mainz presented him to the people assembled in the church, with these words: 'This is he who has been chosen by God, designated by our late lord and king, Henry, and who has been raised to the throne by all the princes, the noble Lord Otto. If the choice pleases you, raise your right hands.' The people all raised their hands. It was a last remnant of the old custom of election by the whole tribe, and not by the chiefs alone."—*Duruy.* Then he was led to the altar, where he was given the sword to chastise the enemies of Christ, the mantle of peace, the scepter of power, and after being annointed with oil, received the golden crown of Karl the Great. A great feast followed, and all the dukes served him according to their offices, though many of them, including his own brothers, soon rebelled against him. He proved so brave, wise, and forgiving that he forced them all to submission, and, like his father, was strong enough to hold the German tribes together as one nation. He waged war against the Bohemians, Poles, and Danes, and, following the policy of Charlemagne, attempted to make them at once Christians, and subjects of his empire. Wishing to re-establish the Holy Roman Empire of Charlemagne, Otto crossed the Alps at the head of an army, and without much opposition received at Milan the crown of the Lombards, and at Rome that of the Cæsars. Henceforth the kings of Germany claimed to be the kings of Lombardy and Roman emperors, and felt it the greatest honor to be head of Christendom and guardian of the faith of the Catholic Church. In protecting their Italian interests the emperors wasted German blood and treasure that should have been devoted to Germany. They were often absent for years, and meanwhile the dukes and counts became almost sovereign princes. From this it may easily be understood that Germany remained a group of almost independent states until 1871 (see Modern History), instead of growing into a united nation like other European peoples.—*Adapted.*

The controversy which arose between the Pope and the German emperors resulted during the Crusades in the triumph of the papacy. (See story of "Frederick Barbarossa," Third Crusade.)

THE CRUSADES.

CONDITION OF THE WORLD BEFORE THE FIRST CRUSADE.

"Within this world of the Middle Ages, there were two entirely distinct worlds—that of the Gospel and that of the Koran. They had already come sometimes into collision; but, finding that they were nearly equal in strength, they had been content with tacitly dividing the known world between them. The Koran ruled from the Pyrenees to the mouth of the Ganges; the Gospels ruled the whole of Europe, with the exception of Spain. Only the two outer edges of these two worlds had come into contact with each other in the frontier wars, but the time had now come when they were to be involved in a general war."—*Duruy*.

Throughout Christendom the German spirit prevailed. A system of society essentially German in character had rescued Europe from chaos and anarchy, and was now attaining its complete development. That system was feudalism. "Feudal castles, defended by rampart and moat, crowned every height, and feudal knights, wearing chain mail, bestriding mettled steeds, and attended by mounted spearmen, rode about, imposing awe alike on priests and crowned kings, on peasants occupied with tillage and burghers engaged in trade."— *Edgar*.

We have said all of Europe was thus ruled, but we have lost sight of that remote corner of Christendom— the remains of the Empire of the East, which dragged out a barren and insignificant existence, like an island surrounded by the floods of invasion. "The separation between the Empire of the East and the German peoples had become even wider, since it had become a religious separation also." The Greek church was the original Christian church, and was the source and background of the Western. Christianity arose in the East, and Greek was the language of the Scriptures and the early services of the church. When the old Roman empire fell in two, the Greek Church became separate in government, interest, and ideas from the Western. The Greek Church is ruled by bishops and does not acknowledge the supremacy of the Pope. A disputed point in the creed and some differences in observances, such as the use of leavened instead of unleavened bread, and the marriage of the priests, led to a complete separation of the churches in 1054.—*Adapted from Britannica and Duruy's "Middle Ages."*

Though separated from the rest of Christendom, the Empire of the East had repelled repeated attacks of the Russians and Bulgarians from the north until the former wished a peaceful alliance. After the marriage of their chief with the daughter of the emperor (980 A. D.), peace reigned between the two peoples, and Christianity became introduced into Russia. The principal Greek churches of to-day are those of Russia and Greece.

As before related, the Greeks lost all their territory in Asia Minor in the first great attack of the Arabs, in the seventh century. In the tenth century, however, the Greek army not only regained Cilicia and Syria, but went still farther, crossing the Euphrates and striking terror into the heart of Bagdad.—*Adapted from Duruy.*

Invasion by Turks.—The Arabian empire was now in a

decline, and a new and formidable enemy was about to appear. The Turks, who have been introduced before, as the body-guard of the Caliph of Bagdad, now came in hordes across the Oxus. "Their flocks and herds were their only riches; their tents, either black or white, were covered with felt and of a circular form; their winter apparel was sheep-skin; a robe of cotton, their summer garment; the features of the men were harsh and ferocious; the countenance of the women soft and pleasing. Their wandering life maintained the free exercise of arms; they fought on horseback." "The Turkish slaves, who aspired to the throne of Bagdad, encouraged these emigrations, which recruited their armies, awed their subjects and rivals, and protected the frontier of the Arabian Empire," as the Goths did that of the Romans. Their numbers may well be understood by the following story: The sultan had inquired of a chief what supply of men he could furnish for military service. "If you send," replied the chief, "one of these arrows into our camp, fifty thousand of your servants will mount on horseback." "And if that number," continued the sultan, "should not be sufficient?" "Send this second arrow to the horde of Balik, and you will find fifty thousand more." "But," said the sultan, dissembling his anxiety, "if I should stand in need of the whole force of your kindred tribes?" "Dispatch my bow," was the last reply of Ismael, "and as it is circulated around, the summons will be obeyed by two hundred thousand horse." The apprehension of such formidable friendship led the sultan to transport the most obnoxious tribes where they would be separated from their brethren by the river Oxus and enclosed on all sides by obedient cities.

As the Arab power declined, these barbarous tribes overran Persia, and gradually adopted the dress, language, and refinement of the Persians. The most deserving of the Arabians and Persians were promoted to the honors of the state; and the whole body of the Turkish nation embraced, with fervor and sincerity, the religion of Mahomet. In 1071 the victorious Turks conquered Armenia and captured the Greek Emperor, Romanus Diogenes. Their dominion soon extended from the borders of China to the Bosporus and Mediterranean.

Jerusalem was taken about 1076, and the Arabian governors retired into Egypt.—*Adapted from Gibbon.*

Pilgrimages to Jerusalem.—"Under Constantine I, in the fourth century A. D., Christianity arose from the cross to wear the crown of the world. Temples and churches covered the holy places of Jerusalem, Bethlehem, and Nazareth." "A pilgrimage to Jerusalem, or other hallowed spots, became the most popular of penances. In the general belief, to atone for the greatest sin, one had only to bathe in the Jordan or spend a night on Calvary.

"The pilgrims increased in number, and at last St. Helena, mother of Constantine, at the age of seventy-eight, visited the holy places and discovered what was supposed to be the wood of the true cross." "She rendered her visit memorable by founding the Church of the Nativity at Bethlehem, and Constantine, influenced by his mother's example, built a magnificent church on the site of the Holy Sepulcher."—*Edgar and Zigzag Journey.*

"No sooner had the war-like Germans and Northmen been converted from the worship of Thor and Odin to a knowledge of the truth, than they became eager to visit those places where their Redeemer had taught and suffered, made the blind to see and the lame to walk, restored life to the dead, and given hope to the living. The roads to Zion were crowded with pilgrims eager to worship at the Sepulcher; Jerusalem became the seat of a patriarch; new and splendid churches were erected; monasteries sprung up on the banks of rivers and on the sides of mountains; and thousands of Europeans remained in Palestine to devote their lives to works of beneficence and charity.

Conquest by Persians.—"But evil days were at hand. At the beginning of the seventh century the Persians, who had long been formidable foes of the Eastern Empire, penetrated to Palestine, took the Holy City by storm and destroyed the church of the Holy Sepulcher. After shedding much blood and doing much mischief, they withdrew, carrying with them the true cross, the patriarch, and many of the principal inhabitants. After ten years of mourning and woe, however, the scene changed, and the Greek Emperor, Heraclius, triumphing over his pagan foes, brought back the surviving captives. Deeming the true cross by far the most glorious of his trophies, the Emperor entered the city walking barefoot, and carrying the sacred relic on his shoulders."

The sacred edifices were now repaired and everything seemed prosperous, the Christians congratulating themselves that their troubles were at an end. But at this period, as we already know, a new race of conquerors arose to influence the world.

Conquest by Arabs.—In 636 the Caliph Omar entered Jerusalem on his rough-haired camel, and the city was now under Mohammedan rule. The presence of the Moslem rulers in Syria and Palestine did not prevent pilgrimages to the Holy Sepulcher. "Haroun-al-Raschid, the most famous of the caliphs at Bagdad, prompted by respect for the name of Charlemagne, regarded them with favor, and treated them with kindness. All pilgrims to the city, without danger, found entertainment in a hospital, surrounded by gardens and vineyards, and many found a resting place in a cemetery, shaded with trees, near the fountain of Shiloh." About the middle of the tenth century the caliphs of Cairo obtained possession of Syria. They, feeling anxious to enrich their dominions, encouraged pilgrimages for the sake of the gold and silver received in exchange for relics and consecrated trinkets. "During the first five decades of the eleventh century, saints and sinners flocked from the west to Jerusalem. A belief prevailed in Europe that the 'second coming of Christ' was at hand. People of all ranks, in hopes of atoning for their sins, rushed to the east. The caliphs, glad to replenish their treasury, demanded a piece of gold from every one who entered the gates of Jerusalem, and, as most of the Christians left home with nothing but their script and staff, the exaction of this tribute proved most cruel." But these trials were slight compared with the persecutions which were yet to be visited upon them.

Conquest by Turks.—"Entering where Roman, and Persian, and Arabian had come before them, the Turks slaughtered and devastated without the slightest distinction. Mosques and churches were given up to pillage, and the blood of Christian and Egyptain flowed in the same stream.

"With ferocious foes in Jerusalem and ferocious foes in Asia Minor, Christians in the East found their plight deplorable. When Peter the Hermit turned his thoughts toward Palestine, matters had come to the worst. Christians were beaten with rods, loaded with chains, sold as slaves, and harnessed like oxen. Never had they felt so much misery, never had they entertained so little hope, as when Peter the Hermit took the cross at Amiens, France, and turned his steps eastward to worship at the Holy Sepulcher."—*Compiled from Edgar.*

THE FIRST CRUSADE.

Peter the Hermit.—"One day in the year 1094, when the Conquest of England by the Normans had inspired feudal warriors with a desire for adventurous expeditions, a little man, mounted on a mule, might have been observed to ascend the heights of Emmaus, and come in sight of Jerusalem. The appearance of the rider was most eccentric; indeed the woolen mantle gathered round his person, the thick cord that girded his waist, the monk's hood thrown over his head, and the sandals on his feet, formed a costume so grotesque as to attract notice wherever he appeared. But the rider, Peter the Hermit, was probably in no mood to notice criticism;

for his soul must have glowed with ardor as he ambled onwards to the Holy City.

"Jerusalem could no longer have been described the most glorious city of the East. Formed of mosques, and churches, and square houses, surmounted by flat terraces, situated on four hills, encircled by a strong wall which undulated with the uneven ground, and surrounded by sterile plains and barren mountains, where a few thorns and olives struggled into growth, and where a solitary palm-tree, here and there, stood erect, the city presented an aspect suggestive of mournful reflections. The fervor of the Hermit was aroused to the highest pitch when he gazed with entranced eye on Zion and Olivet, and on Moriah, where the site of the Temple was occupied by Omar's mosque, and on Calvary, where the Church of the Resurrection stood as a monument of Constantine's piety."—*Edgar.*

Taking up his abode under the roof of a Latin Christian, he heard recited the woes endured by the Christians until his blood boiled. He occupied himself with meditating schemes for their relief. At length, one day, when prostrated before the Holy Sepulcher, a celestial voice seemed to call to him: "Arise, Peter; go forth to proclaim the tribulations of my people, for the time has come when they must be protected and this Holy Sepulcher wrested from the hands of the infidel." Filled with enthusiastic faith by these words, Peter believed himself to be the chosen deliverer of Jerusalem, and immediately repaired to the house of the patriarch. Simeon, who now held that office, was a man advanced in life, with white hair and venerable figure. But neither his age nor sacred office had protected him from insults and injuries. In a voice devoid of hope, the patriarch recited the sufferings of his people, and bewailed the fate of the holy city. "But is there no remedy?" cried Peter. "Must these calamities continue without redress?" Slowly and sadly the patriarch responded: "These sufferings are plainly the visitation of a most wise God upon a sinful people, and there is no earthly help." "O, let me but rouse the Christian warriors of the West, and Jerusalem may yet be free," exclaimed the excited Peter "If they but knew of your miseries they would come to your aid. Write then to the pope and to the Latin Christians and affix your seal to the epistle. I will do penance for my sins by traveling through the West to raise an army for your cause."

Gathering hope from these stirring words of Peter, the patriarch shed tears of joy, and immediately prepared the letters, imploring aid from the pope and the Western Christians. Without delay Peter set out on his mission, which was to influence the destinies of Europe and Asia for centuries to come.

Arriving at Rome, Peter gained an audience with Pope Urban the Second. The pope listened to his appeal with favor, and, regarding him as a prophet, commissioned him to arouse the warriors of Europe

Preaching the First Crusade.—Never did enthusiast meet greater success in convincing his hearers. Crossing the Alps into France, he electrified city, town, castle, and hamlet with his eloquence. He recited the pitiful tale of the patriarch; how the devout believers were spurned and insulted at the very tomb of Christ, and whenever it pleased the bloody-minded followers of the prophet, they were thrown into prison, beaten, and even put to death. Would not the Princes of the West go to their rescue and deliver the Holy Sepulcher out of the hands of the savage Turk? Wherever Peter the Hermit preached—in the churches, at the market places, or under a tree by the wayside, the people revered him as a saint, and crowded around him, deeming themselves happy to touch the hem of his garment or pluck a hair from the mane of his mule. His fame even crossed the channel, and Saxon and Norman alike were fired with zeal.

While Peter was arousing Christendom to arm for the recovery of the Holy Sepulcher, the pope received letters from Alexis, the Greek emperor, imploring his assistance, and that of the Western Princes. He pointed out the dangers which would befall Christianity if Constantinople were captured by the Turk, and offered bountiful rewards for the services rendered. From this appeal it was evident that the Greeks no longer possessed courage and strength enough to fight their own battles.

Council at Clermont.—The pope now convoked a council at Clermont, in France, which was attended by three hundred bishops and a multitude of princes and nobles of the West. Though it was winter time, the pope crossed the Alps to preside and found Clermont a vast camp. The city itself was crowded with princes, prelates, and ambassadors; the neighboring towns and villages were filled to overflowing, and in spite of the severity of the weather, thousands were encamped in pavilions and tents in the meadows and fields.

Pope Urban, accompanied by Peter the Hermit, and attended by cardinals, ascended a throne and related the miseries of the faithful at Jerusalem and the desecration of the holy places. "Christian warriors," said Urban, addressing the assembled multitude, "rejoice, for you, who without ceasing seek vain pretexts for war, have to-day found true ones. You are not now called to avenge the injuries of men, but injuries offered to God; and it is not now a town or a castle that will reward your valor, but the wealth of Asia, and a land flowing with milk and honey. If you triumph over your foes, the kingdoms of the East will be your heritage. If you are conquered, you will have the glory of dying where Christ died. This is the time to prove that you are animated by a true courage, and to expiate so many violences committed in the bosom of peace. When Christ summons you to His defense, let no base affections detain you at home—listen to nothing but the groans of Jerusalem, and remember that the Lord hath said: 'He that will not take up the cross and follow me is unworthy of me.'"

At first the multitude listened in solemn silence to the words of the pope, then broke forth into sobs as he pictured the cruelties practiced at Jerusalem.

"Will you not drive out the handmaid and her children," continued the pope, "lest they increase in power and Europe be threatened by these enemies of Christ? Gird your swords to your thighs, ye men of might; it is our part to pray, and it is yours to fight—ours, with Moses, to hold up unwearied hands; yours to stretch forth the sword against the children of Amelek."

"God wills it!" shouted with one accord the enthusiastic multitude, as they surged about the speaker with excited faces and uplifted swords.

"God indeed wills it," responded the pope. "Go forth, brave warriors of the cross; and let 'God wills it' be your watchword and battle cry in the holy war."

A loud cry of "God wills it!" again broke from the tumultuous crowd; but, at a gesture from the pope, silence fell upon the great assembly and stern warriors bent their knees, as the cardinal pronounced a form of confession for those who would enlist in the holy enterprise.

Thereupon a noted bishop stepped forward to receive the sacred badge of the cross and take the oath of loyalty to Christ. Following his example, knights and barons now crowded around the pope, that they might receive the red cross and enter the way of God. All who took the oath stitched the red cross upon the right shoulder of the mantle and became soldiers of the cross—or Crusaders. Entire remission of sins was granted to all taking part in the holy war, which was called the Crusade.

The council was then dissolved, the pope continuing his preaching throughout France, the knights repairing to their castles to prepare for the expedition, which all agreed should take place the following spring. Already France resounded with the din of preparation. From Scandinavia to the Mediterranean, men of all classes assumed the cross and could scarcely be restrained from setting out in mid-winter.—*Adapted from Edgar.*

Mustering of the Crusaders.—The nobles mortgaged their estates and with the money thus raised equipped armies for the Holy War. Among the foremost of these was Godfrey of Bouillon, Duke of Lorraine, a prince renowned for piety, learning, and courage. It was in his father's house that Peter the Hermit had lived as a retainer before he became a monk. No prince in Europe had a more enviable position than Godfrey. A lord of many castles, of vast fortune, and of spotless reputation, yet all these advantages failed to secure happiness. Memory was constantly recalling scenes in which he had taken a prominent part which no longer met the approval of his conscience. In his early life he had fought under the banner of Henry IV, King of Germany, against the pope. During the siege of Rome it was Godfrey who, first of the imperial captains, broke over the ramparts and opened the gates of the city. Filled with remorse as he reflected on this sinful revolt against the head of the Church, he now eagerly assumed the cross, hoping to atone for the sins of his rash youth by giving his life, if need be, in recovering the Holy Land from the infidels.

He proceeded to sell or mortgage his castles and estates; he transferred his cities and principalities, gave up his duchy, that he might deprive himself of every temptation to return. With the money obtained, he arrayed a magnificent army of ten thousand knights, the flower of European chivalry, while a force of eighty thousand foot made up the body of his army. His principal officers were his two brothers, Eustace and Baldwin, his kinsman, Baldwin du Bourg, with many knights and nobles of less distinction.

While Godfrey was assembling his forces by the Meuse and Moselle, the warriors in the south of France were rallied to the cross by Raymond, Count of Toulouse. Though an aged soldier with whitened locks, his ardor was not diminished, and he aroused himself to take part in the enterprise. "In my youth," he said, "I fought the Saracens in Spain, and, in my old age, I will go and fight them in Asia." The Bishop of Puy, who was first to assume the cross at the council of Clermont, accompanied Raymond of Toulouse, and a hundred thousand men of Gascony and Provence flocked to the old count's standard.

Meanwhile Hugh of Vermandois, brother of the King of France; Robert of Flanders; Stephen, Count of Blois; and Robert, Count of Paris, also rallied their knights and retainers and made ready for the march into Asia. All Normandy was kindled by the crusading fervor.

The court of Rouen furnished two gallant leaders. These were Robert Short Hose, son of William the Conqueror, and Edgar Atheling, heir of the Saxon line in England.

Robert Short Hose possessed all the elements of a genuine crusader—brave, rash, fanatical, so improvident that he was often reduced to a state of ridiculous poverty. Indeed, the chronicler states that he was frequently prevented from leaving his bed and attending mass for want of decent clothes. Excluded from the English throne by his younger brother, William Rufus, the situation of

Curthose was not enviable. The prospect of escaping from his creditors was too tempting to be resisted. William Rufus, rejoicing to hear of his brother's intention of leaving Europe, readily furnished the sum of ten thousand marks, and Curthose gave a mortgage over Normandy for five years. When he set up his white banner embroidered with gold, multitudes came to join a leader so generous and brave.

Different Routes.—The pilgrim princes appointed Constantinople as a rendezvous, and agreed to set out at different dates and to pursue different routes. The countries through which they were to pass were already half exhausted by the ravages and excesses of the vanguard of the Crusade, led by Walter the Penniless and Peter the Hermit, and that rabble which recognized the leadership of a goat and a goose. (See accounts in Ridpath's, Edgar's, Duruy's, and Barnes's histories.) They therefore commenced their expedition eastward, all grandly arrayed. Godfrey's armies passed through Germany and Hungary. The men of Southern France, led by Robert of Toulouse, crossed the Alps and passed through Dalmatia and Thrace. Robert Short Hose and the Count of Blois, of Flanders, and of Vermandois, went to join the Normans of Italy, who were led by Bohemond, Prince of Tarentum, and his nephew, Tancred, who, next to Godfrey, was the most perfect knight of the times. These together crossed the Adriatic and passed through Greece and Macedonia.

Every warrior wore a casque and hauberk of chain mail. . The infantry carried long shields, the cavalry round bucklers for their defense, and a goodly supply of swords, lances, poniards, axes, maces, bows, slings, and cross-bows, with which to pursue the work of carnage and destruction. Knights and nobles, grooms and squires were equally unaware of the obstacles to be encountered. Many of the warriors took with them their wives and children, and rode along with bugles at their girdles, hawks on their wrists, and hounds running by their side. They seem to have considered the Crusade as a sort of pleasant excursion, and to have anticipated reaching the Holy City, if not without fighting battles, at least without storming fortresses. (Tennyson's "Bugle Song.")

The rabble vanguard of the soldiers of the cross had not left a favorable impression upon the Greeks at Constantinople. We can imagine with what dismay the Emperor Alexis heard the news, that vast armies composed of the bravest warriors of France were marching toward his capital on their way to encounter the Saracens.

He began to repent of having implored their aid, for now they seemed as formidable as the Turk. He knew only too well the corruption of his own heart, the insecurity of his throne, and the cupidity of his enemies. If those bold Northmen should attempt to seize his dominions he realized that his army of mercenaries was no match for the mail-clad warriors of Godfrey and Raymond. He therefore resolved to depend upon artful craft.

While Alexis was forming his plans, it happened that Hugh of Vermandois, brother of the king of France, was shipwrecked on the shore of Epirus. Alexis, perceiving his opportunity, ordered Count Hugh to be seized and brought to Constantinople as a hostage for the good conduct of his comrades, the Crusaders. Godfrey of Bouillon, having learned of this act of treachery on his arrival in Thrace, dispatched messengers to demand the count's freedom. An unsatisfactory answer was returned by the emperor, and soon a crowd of flying Greeks brought word into the capital that the Crusaders were ravaging the country and treating the Greeks as enemies. In alarm Alexis sent to promise satisfaction, and Godfrey bade his warriors refrain from further injury to the Greeks. But the army of the Crusaders had no sooner reached the gates of the city, when Alexis closed the gates and conceived the idea of starving them into submission. The result which might have been expected followed. The Crusaders burst into the suburbs of the city, plundered palaces and villages, captured storehouses, and helped themselves bountifully to whatever good things the fruitful East had heaped up in her lap. Alexis, soon perceiving that he had adopted the wrong policy, sent a messenger to Godfrey, promising to supply the army out of stores of the city; then, with some reluctance, the Crusaders refrained from pillaging. Notwithstanding the outward show of friendship that now existed between the two races, quarrels were of frequent occurrence. The Greeks regarded the Franks as barbarians, the Franks taunted the Greeks with being unable to fight their own battles.

Crusaders at Constantinople.—The emperor within the walls was kept in continual alarm by the threatening aspect of the crusading host. He now set his heart on a new scheme, which he hoped would avert the mischief. He determined to demand homage of these Western princes encamped outside of his gates, so that they would be compelled to fight for his interests. Such oaths of fealty, if once given, could not be honorably or even decently violated. Having secured such an oath from Hugh, who was still a prisoner, he was confident of success with the other princes. It was only by sending his son to the Crusaders' camp as hostage that he gained the consent of Godfrey, Robert Short Hose, and the counts of Flanders and Blois (Bohemond and Tancred had not yet arrived). Raymond of Toulouse scornfully refused, saying, "I have not come to the East to seek a master."

Wishing to impress the Crusaders with the majesty of his court, at a day appointed, he received the princes in his imperial palace. He hoped by superficial magnificence to conceal the real weakness of his empire, and did not perceive that those who bent the knee before his throne had a perfect contempt for his power. While the emperor was presenting the Crusaders with rich gifts, a slight incident awoke him from his delusive dream.

Count Robert of Paris, feeling such disdain for the mummery that was enacting, could not refrain from showing his contempt. Just when the ceremonies were intended to be most impressive, this stalwart son of the ancient sea-kings strode boldly forward to the throne and sat down beside the emperor. At this the Greeks were horrified, and the Crusaders laughed. Some of the more prudent Franks remonstrated, one of them saying, as he pulled Count Robert by the arm, "When you are in a foreign country, you should observe its customs." "Truly," exclaimed Robert, glancing mockingly toward Alexis, "but this is a pleasant clown, who is seated, while so many noble captains are standing." The emperor was obliged to overlook the insult, and when the ceremony was over he attempted to engage the stubborn Crusader in pleasant conversation. "What is your birth and which is your country?" said he, with a mild accent, to the surly Robert. "I am a Frenchman," said the Frank, "and of the highest rank of nobles. And one thing I know, that in my country there is a place near a church where those repair who are eager to attest their valor. I have often been there myself, and no one has ventured to present himself before me." The hint of a challenge was lost on the mild mannered Alexis, who had as little notion of hazarding his person as of resigning his throne.

Soon after this event Bohemond and Tancred, with thirty thousand men, joined the Crusaders. Bohemond, a native of Italy, but Norman to the backbone, was brave, accomplished, but utterly unscrupulous. He fought with courage, spoke with eloquence, but without regard either to conscience or God. Tarentum was far too small a place for so ambitious a spirit, and it was with enthusiasm that he joined the Franks at Constantinople. He recommended to Godfrey the seizure of the Empire of the East, but Godfrey reminded him that they were soldiers of the cross going to deliver Jerusalem, and that their duty as Christians was not to attack the Greeks but to vanquish the pagans. It was with the greatest dread that Alexis heard of the arrival of Bohemond, but by cunning and bribery he succeeded in winning from him also a promise of homage.

The entire year of 1096 was consumed in the gathering together of the armies before the walls of Constantinople. At length, in May of '97, to the extreme satisfaction of Alexis, the crusading army of a hundred thousand mounted knights and five hundred thousand footmen crossed into Asia Minor. "At the head rode the austere Godfrey, the white-haired Raymond of Toulouse, and Peter the Hermit, mounted on a mule. Priest, matron and maid still journeyed by the side of young warriors, who carried white hawks on their wrists and whistled to hounds."

Siege of Nice.—Soon they reached the city of Nice in Bithynia. The sultan had placed his wife, his children, and his treasures within the walls, confident in the strong fortifications, while he encamped with the Turkish army on the neighboring mountains. Here lay a powerful city, surrounded by strong walls, protected by hundreds of towers; a ditch broad and deep enclosed the fortifications, and a lake washed its foundations, and communicated with the sea.

The Crusaders commenced the siege with zeal and courage, flinging themselves against the walls of the city in an impetuous assault. Seeing that they were not successful, the sultan and his army charged down from the mountain sides. Such was the fury of the attack, that the soldiers under Raymond of Toulouse, who were stationed so as to bear the brunt of the battle, were thrown into some disorder, but were quickly rallied by their brave leader. Robert Short Hose and Robert of Flanders, hastening to the rescue, soon compelled the sultan to sound his bugles for retreat. Now the Crusaders commenced a systematic siege of the city. A Lombard engineer skillfully constructed the war machines, necessary in the Middle Ages in conducting the siege of fortified cities. With the aid of these, they battered the ramparts, hurled masses of stone and blocks of wood with a crash into the city, fought the besieged in a hand-to-hand fight from the summits of high towers wheeled up to the ramparts.

Meanwhile the Saracens were likewise defiantly hurling darts, stones, blocks of wood, and boiling tar upon the heads of their assailants. One gigantic Saracen was conspicuous during the siege, hurling darts, arrows and stones with unerring aim. He grew so bold as to stand upright on the walls and challenge the Crusaders. Hundreds of arrows were immediately directed toward him, but without avail, for he seemed to bear a charmed life. At length Godfrey of Bouillon seized a cross-bow, took aim, and the next moment the boastful Saracen fell, pierced through the heart.

After the siege had been carried on for several weeks, it became evident that the city could never be taken, while the besieged received supplies across the lake. Accordingly, in the dead of night, the Crusaders succeeded in launching their boats on the lake and captured the wife and children of the sultan as they were attempting to escape. The next morning the besieged, with dismay, discovered that their foes had captured the lake, and that the family of the sultan had been taken prisoners.

Now the Crusaders expected an easy conquest, but the crafty Alexis had planned otherwise. Pretending to accompany the Crusaders as an ally, he had adroitly dispatched messengers to the Saracens persuading them that it would be greatly to their advantage to surrender to him, rather than to place themselves at the mercy of the Franks. Just as they were preparing a final assault, what was their astonishment to see the standard of the Greek emperor displayed from turret and tower. Mortified and angered at this double dealing, they could only smother their wrath as Alexis attempted to pacify them by praising their valor and distributing valuable gifts. As soon as possible they took up their march toward Jerusalem, feeling the greatest hatred and contempt for the monarch to whom they had paid homage.

Journey Continued.—The army marched in two divisions that they might better procure provisions in the country through which they passed. The larger of these was headed by Godfrey of Bouillon, Raymond of Toulouse, and the Counts of Vermandois and Flanders. The other, composed mostly of Normans, was led by Bohemond of Tarentum, Tancred, and Robert Short Hose.

Valley of Dogorgan.—The division under Bohemond followed the margin of a river into th lley of Dogorgan, where they found a tempting p ace to encamp. Here was a beautiful stream of water, plenty of pasture, and, near by, an abundance of timber. Bohemond called a halt, the heralds, according to custom, shouted three time, "God save the Holy Sepulcher!" the Crusaders pitched their tents, tethered their horses, partook of what refreshments they had, and, as darkness over-

shadowed the valley, took their needed repose. The
night passed away in peace, but, by break of day, news
was brought into the camp by the Greeks that the sultan
with a powerful army was right upon them. Springing
upon their feet they perceived a cloud of dust in the distance, which announced without doubt the coming of
the foe.

Bohemond with skill and coolness fortified the camp
with wagons and palisades, placing the women, children,
and wounded in the center and a guard of soldiers around
it. The cavalry he sent forward under Tancred and
Robert Short Hose to dispute the passage of the river,
while he with a few followers mounted some rising
ground that he might watch the progress of the battle
and issue suitable orders. These preparations were none
too soon, for the Moslem host in their white turbans,
green vests, and armed with long spears, approached,
blowing their horns, beating drums, and filling the air
with their fearful yells. At the same time they discharged volleys of arrows and darts upon the Crusaders.
These missiles rattled off the linked mail of the knights,
doing no injury, but the spirited horses, stung by the
javelins and unused to the drums and yells of the Saracens, grew restive, plunged and reared until their riders
were in danger of being unhorsed. The knights, rendered desperate by the showers of arrows and the fierce
glare of the sun, plunged into the stream and rushed
upon their assailants, thinking to come to a hand-to-hand fight.

But the Saracens had no such intention. They opened
their ranks to the Christian warriors, retreated to a safe

distance, charged again with all the speed of their Arab horses, let fly a shower of arrows, and again sped out of reach.

The Crusaders were thrown into disorder by this unusual warfare. Saddle after saddle was emptied, and horses, without riders, running hither and thither, increased the confusion. In vain Tancred and Count Robert of Paris threw themselves into the melee. Count Robert fell mortally wounded, after seeing forty of his followers killed. Tancred was about to be overpowered, when Bohemond rushed to the rescue and bore his nephew off to a place of safety.

Meanwhile, the sultan and a body of choice horsemen descended upon the camp, scattering the guard and bringing terror to the hearts of the women and children and priests. Curthose, who had prudently refrained from crossing the river, bore down upon them, sounding his war-cry of "God wills it!" and followed by a host of knights, he cut down the principal Saracens with his sword. Bohemond, hearing of the peril to the camp, charged to the rescue with such force that the Saracens were soon expelled.

Notwithstanding the success of this onset and the valor inspired by the courage of Curthose and Bohemond, the prospect was most alarming. The Crusaders, driven back upon the camp, were but a handful compared with the overwhelming numbers of the Saracen host. The remaining warriors, almost prostrated by the intense heat, suffocated by the dust, and parched with thirst, were unfit for further conflict; the horses, tired, wounded, and bleeding, were too weak to carry their riders.

In despair, the Crusaders gave up all hope of seeing Jerusalem. Bohemond alone tried to keep up their courage, with the hope that Godfrey's division would come to their rescue. His words had very little effect; women bewailed their fate, priests implored divine aid, and soldiers, on their knees, entreated the priests to grant them absolution.

Suddenly a joyful shout rang through the camp, as the shrill bugles of Godfrey were heard in the distance, and fifty thousand sabers flashed in the sunlight on the summit of the hills behind the camp. The sultan now thought it prudent to retire to the opposite mountains, apparently not anticipating pursuit. In this he was mistaken. As soon as Godfrey arrived he formed his men in line of battle, ready for the assault. Priests passed along the lines, exhorting them to remember the Holy Sepulcher, and bestowing upon all the blessing of the church. When the command of "Forward!" was given, every man advanced with the cry of "God wills it!"

The soldiers of Raymond of Toulouse were the first to meet the foe, and such was the impetuosity of their attack that the Saracen line was broken. Meanwhile they found themselves attacked on one flank by Bohemond and Curthose; on the other by Godfrey and the Count of Flanders. Now all was disorder, and, to complete the rout, the Bishop of Puy, who had charge of the reserve, appeared from behind a hill and attacked their rear. So surrounded were the Saracens, that they could scarcely hope to escape; but, moved by desperation, some fought their way out through woods and over rocks.

Thousands of turbaned Moslems fell on the mountain sides; and the sultan, seeing all was lost, fled from the scene of action, though continuing to affirm that he had won the victory.

The successful Crusaders now proceeded to the camp of the enemy, where they found a rich booty to reward their valor. Here, indeed, were the treasures of the East: a bountiful supply of provisions; jewels which the enemy, in their haste, had abandoned; camels, with which the Western warriors were wholly unacquainted; and tents, the magnificence of which excited their admiration.

In triumph they returned to their own camp laden with booty, the priests marching before, singing hymns of praise, the camels and horses which had been their prey bringing up the rear.

But the joy was not unalloyed, for many were mourning the loss of brothers and kinsmen. As many as four thousand Christians had perished in that morning's struggle. It was the general belief, however, that the souls of those who fell with arms in their hands and the cross on their shoulders were purified from all sin and their names at once enrolled in the army of martyrs.

The Desert.—The army now moved forward in a body toward Antioch, but soon encountered new difficulties. The sultan, to gratify his desire for revenge, had laid waste the country, so that it was a barren desert, offering no food for men and no fodder for horses. Subsisting on roots and stray ears of corn, the utmost distress prevailed. Hawks drooped and died, hounds ran off in search of food, delicate women and robust warriors fell by the way. Finally the scarcity of water was added to famine. No spring nor stream nor pond could be found to slake their burning thirst. At length, when the whole host seemed about to perish, the hounds came into the camp with wet skins and paws covered with sand. Following their footprints the Crusaders found a river. The pilgrims rushed to it in a mass, and such was their frenzy that they threw themselves into the water and drank to excess, so that hundreds died on the banks and others became too sick to continue the journey. In the midst of this suffering the cry of "On to Jerusalem!" resounded through the camp, and the toilsome march was renewed. About the middle of October the half-starved pilgrims entered a mountain pass, which led them into a region of plenty. On every side were towns and fields, which furnished supplies in abundance. The strength of the Crusaders revived and they pressed on to the city of Antioch, which rose to their vision.—*Adapted from Edgar.*

Antioch.—"Antioch was known as the 'Queen of the East,' and seemed not unworthy of the name. A beautiful situation, a lofty castle, magnificent edifices, and strong walls, fortified by four hundred and sixty towers, gave a dignified and picturesque aspect to the city. On the north rose one mountain covered with houses and gardens; on the south another mountain celebrated for its forests and springs. The suburbs, which boasted of the fountain of Daphne, were fair to look upon; the ramparts were washed by the river Orontes, which communicated with a lake abounding in fish, and, at a few miles' distance, flowed into the sea. The city itself could not fail to be of interest to the Crusaders; but better than the natural beauty and opulence were the hallowed associations of Antioch. Here the followers of Christ had first taken the name of Christians. Here St. Peter was made first bishop of the church. Here the early saints and martyrs had performed their miracles, and given to the city a sanctity second only to that of Jerusalem."—*Edgar.*

While the main body of the Christian army had been moving toward Antioch, several successes had been obtained by the other divisions. Tancred and Baldwin of Bouillon had captured Tarsus. Tancred also seized Alexandretta, while Baldwin made himself master of Edessa on the Euphrates, and, by marriage with an Armenian princess, obtained possession of the richest provinces of ancient Assyria. The principal cities of Asia Minor had already come under the dominion of the cross, so it was with a most confident spirit that the assembled armies stationed themselves before Antioch.

Siege of Antioch.—They must first capture the bridge across the Orentes. Though it was defended by iron towers, with Curthose leading the van, every obstacle gave way, and the defenders of the bridge were driven within the walls of the city. As they approached the ramparts, strangely enough no foes presented themselves. Judging from this that it would be an easy task to vanquish an enemy so cowardly, they decided "to eat, drink, and be merry." Then it was that the Christian army brought disgrace upon itself. No town nor village nor orchard was safe from their depredations. The soldiers and many of the bishops abandoned themselves to pleasure. While off their guard many of their number were cut off by a sally from the city. The Crusaders, roused to fury, made a hopeless attack on the walls, for they possessed no scaling ladders nor machines.

Finding action a necessity, they now set to work in earnest to besiege the city; but now the consequences of their imprudence came upon them. Although winter was coming on, no supplies had been laid by. Curthose and Bohemond scoured the neighborhood and brought back but little; famine stared them in the face, terrible rainstorms flooded the camp, and gusts of wind destroyed their tents; their clothing was in rags, and many were prostrated with fever. Such was their despair that some abandoned the camp and started out secretly for home. Among these were Peter the Hermit and Robert Short Hose. Peter was brought back by force, and Curthose returned, when summoned by Godfrey in the name of Christ.

Ships with supplies having arrived off the coast, the soldiers, almost unarmed, rushed off to purchase provisions. When returning they were attacked by the Saracens. Godfrey, Curthose, and Tancred came to the rescue; but at this point a large body of Saracens sallied out from the gates of the city, followed to the bridge by the Prince of Antioch, who assured them that the gates would only be opened to them as victors. The Moslem warriors soon discovered their own inferiority in a hand-to-hand combat with the Crusaders, and made attempts to regain the city; but Godfrey had no idea of letting them escape so easily. A sanguinary battle was then fought, continuing till dark, before the prince would open the gates to admit the fugitives.

After this, the Saracens regarded the Crusaders with awe; but winter passed, and the month of May, 1098, drew to a close without any prospect of a surrender. At last the prospect of seizing the city by strategem was offered.

One of the chief commanders in the defense of the city was an Armenian renegade, who thought to advance his fortunes by surrendering the city. Making his resolution known to Bohemond of Tarentum, that knight, thinking to advance his own interests, eagerly favored the enterprise.

At a council of the Christian princes, he offered to have the gates of the city thrown open, hinting that his reward might be the sovereignty of the city. The chiefs at first disdainfully refused to countenance such a cowardly project, but news having arrived that the sultans of Nice and Mossoul were marching at the head of four hundred thousand Moslems to the relief of Antioch, caused the princes to put aside their scruples and agree that Bohemond should be prince of Antioch, if he would take possession of the city. During a stormy night, when the noise of the wind and rain deafened the sentinels, Bohemond, followed by the other Crusaders, scaled the walls of Antioch, by means of rope ladders, which were let down to them, and threw themselves on the city, crying, "God wills it!"

The Crusaders, reduced to half their original numbers, underwent the same sufferings inside the city that they had to bear outside the walls, for they were besieged by two hundred thousand Turks from Bagdad. Godfrey had his last war horse killed, and despair had settled down upon them, when a priest announced to the leaders of the army that Saint Andrew had revealed to him in his sleep that the spear which pierced the side of Christ was under the high altar of the church, and that the possession of this would give a victory to the Christians. They dug under the altar, found the spear; and the Crusaders, filled with enthusiasm, marched against the Turkish army and cut it into pieces.

Journey Continued.—Instead of starting at once for Jerusalem, they stayed six months longer at Antioch, where great numbers died of the plague. When they finally left the city, of the six hundred thousand who had started, only fifty thousand were left; though it is true that a number of them had settled down in the various cities through which the crusade had passed. Besides, some of them, like the Count of Blois and the Count of Vermandois, returned to Europe. The Crusaders followed along the coast of the Mediterranean, in order to keep in communication with the fleets from Genoa and Pisa, which brought them supplies. In addition to this, as they were passing through the rich valleys of the Lebanon range, they recovered from their suffering and regained their strength. The enthusiasm grew as they approached the Holy City and began to traverse places hallowed by the narratives of the Gospels.—*Adapted from Edgar*.

First View of Jerusalem.—"On the morning of the 29th of May, 1099, they ascended the heights of Emmaus and at dawn came in sight of the Holy City.

" 'Jerusalem! Jerusalem!' shouted all the pilgrims, as

they uncovered their heads and rushed forward in ecstasy.

"Lines of walls, groups of massive towers, and a few olive trees rising from the sterile plain were all that met the thousands of arrested eyes; but the sight was enough. A thrilling and sublime emotion pervaded the army of Crusaders as they gazed on the city they had so earnestly longed to behold; and a voice seemed to sound in the ear of each, saying: 'Put thy shoes from off thy feet, for the place whereon thou standest is holy.' The horsemen sprung from their saddles. Some prostrated themselves and kissed the earth; others walked forward barefoot, and all, shedding penitential tears, renewed the vow they had made before leaving Europe."—*Edgar.* (Song, "Jerusalem the Golden.")

Siege of Jerusalem.—Urged by the eloquence of a hermit living on Mt. Olivet, they resolved to make an immediate assault and trust for victory to the aid of Heaven. Accordingly, without machines of war and scarcely a scaling ladder, they advanced and assailed the walls with hammers and pikes; others, ranged at a distance, annoyed the defenders of the city with slings and bows.

"But the Emir of Jerusalem, whose garrison numbered forty thousand men, was in no yielding mood. Machines placed upon the ramparts discharged every species of missile; and blocks of stone, beams of wood, burning torches, boiling pitch, and Greek fire wrought fearful havoc. Still the Crusaders persevered, and the outer wall fell before their impetuous efforts. The inner wall, however, proved such an impassable barrier, that the Crusaders abandoned the siege until they could prosecute it in a more regular fashion.

"To their great distress, they found that the Saracens had scoured the neighborhood and taken everything in the shape of provender into the city, and cut off the supply of water by choking up the wells and poisoning the cisterns. The fountain of Shiloh, only flowing at intervals, could not suffice for fifty thousand people, and most of the water had to be carried in skins from fountains or rivulets many miles off. Encamped on arid plains and under a burning sun, everybody experienced more or less misery; and, as days passed, men, women, and children gave way to despair. There is only one remedy for this state of things,' said the pilgrim princes —'Jerusalem must be taken.'

"At length, obtaining some provisions and tools from a Genoese fleet that had arrived at Joppa, and some lumber from forests thirty miles distant, they constructed war machines. On the 15th of July, 1099, a general assault was made at early dawn, and three great rolling towers were pushed up against the walls of the city. The onset was impetuous and the shock terrible, for the resistance was as obstinate as the assault was enthusiastic. The engines constructed by the Genoese proved very destructive, but the besieged cased the outside of their walls with bags of chaff, straw, and such pliable matter, which conquered the engines of the Christians by yielding to them. At length the Greek fire of the Saracens, by setting their machines on fire, reduced the Christians to despondency. "At the moment, however, when the Crusaders, fatigued with the weight of their armor, covered with dust and oppressed with heat, leaned on their swords and gave way to despair, a horseman, waving a buckler, appeared on Mt. Olivet.

"'Behold,' cried Godfrey, 'St. George has come again to our aid, and makes a signal for us to enter the Holy City.'

"'God wills it!' cried the Crusaders, as they returned with one accord to the assault."—*Edgar.*

Entrance into Jerusalem.—Pious frenzy now rendered the armed pilgrims irresistible. Amid clouds of flame and smoke and dust, Godfrey forced an entry into the city, and Eustace of Bouillon, with a host of warriors, followed with shouts of victory. Curthose and the Count of Flanders redoubled every effort, and scaled the walls sword in hand. Raymond of Toulouse, opposed by the Emir in person, leaping from his wooden towers to the ramparts, caused the Saracens and their leader to fly before the sweep of his sword.

"Jerusalem now resounded with loud cries of vengeance. The conquerors, under a delusion that they were rendering God service, slaughtered without mercy the enemies of their religion. Thousands upon thousands of the vanquished fell, and for days the blood of Saracens, old and young, flowed like water.

"While swords were clashing and blood was flowing, Godfrey of Bouillon, leaving the scene of carnage, laying down his sword, uncovering his head and baring his feet, walked in a posture of humility to the Church of the Resurrection and prostrated himself on the tomb of Christ. On hearing of the pious chief's act of devotion, the Crusaders hastened to follow his example, and, preceded by the clergy, walked in solemn procession, singing penitential psalms and songs of thanksgiving.

"Ere this ceremony was over, the Christians in Jerusalem emerged from places of concealment and advanced to meet their deliverers. The spectacle touched every heart and brought tears to every eye; but, from among princes and peers, they singled out the figure of the little man clad in the woolen mantle who, five years before, had walked wildly about the Holy City busying his brain with projects for their relief. It was Peter the Hermit, whom they regarded as their liberator, and crowding around him they expressed boundless astonishment that one man should have been able to rouse so many nations and to work so mighty a deliverance."—*Edgar*.

Godfrey Made King.—The Crusaders lost no time in organizing their new conquest. Godfrey was unanimously elected King of Jerusalem, but he would only accept the title of Defender and Baron of the Holy Sepulcher, refusing to wear a crown of gold where the Savior of mankind wore a crown of thorns.

"Immediately after the election of Godfrey, the pilgrim princes attended him in triumph to the Church of the Holy Sepulcher, and the warriors there took an oath to rule according to the laws of honor and justice. Scarely, however, was the ceremony over, when startling intelligence reached Jerusalem. It appeared that a mighty army, under the command of the most renowned of Moslem warriors, had arrived at Ascalon, bent on giving the Crusaders battle."—*Edgar*. (See account of battle, pages 109, 110, 111, Edgar, and page 696, Ridpath.)

Return to Europe.—"After the victory of Ascalon,

almost all the nobles were in haste to return to their own firesides; and, with Godfrey and Tancred, hardly more than 300 knights remained in Jerusalem. [Page 112, Edgar.] The ones who remained, with tears in their eyes, begged those who departed never to forget them, saying: 'Do not forget your brothers whom you leave in exile. When you go back to Europe, arouse in all Christians the desire to visit the holy places which we have delivered, and exhort the warriors to come and fight the infidel nations.' But the enthusiasm of Europe was chilled when so few returned from the enormous number that started, and fifty years elapsed before another crusade of any importance was undertaken to relieve the kingdom founded at Jerusalem."—*Duruy.*

Godfrey's Government.—But the valiant Godfrey did not live long to enjoy the fruits of his toil and warfare. He faithfully discharged his duty as Baron of the Holy Sepulcher, by giving regular institutions to the country and people he had conquered. Tancred was sent into Galilee, where he captured the town of Tiberias. The whole province was added to Godfrey's dominions. When Tancred was attacked by the Saracen army from Damascus, Godfrey went to his assistance, and, after defeating the Moslems, returned by way of Cæsarea. The Emir of that district met him in a friendly way and made him a seemingly courteous offer of fruit. Godfrey, unsuspicious of treachery, ate an apple, and immediately sickened and died on the 18th of July, 1100. His remains were laid to rest, according to his wish, on the slope of Calvary, not far from the Holy Sepulcher. All Christendom heard of the sad event with sorrow.

Baldwin I., King of Jerusalem.—Baldwin of Bouillon, making over his province of Edessa to his kinsman, Baldwin du Bourg, became king of Jerusalem. During his reign and that of his successor, Baldwin du Bourg, the Christian possessions were well defended and increased in extent; but after these kings the decline of the kingdom began. "The Turks of Mosul and Damascus took Edessa and massacred the inhabitants (1147). This bloody disaster, which left Palestine unprotected, impelled Europe to renew the crusade."—*Duruy.*

THE SECOND CRUSADE (1147).

Preaching by St. Bernard.—St. Bernard of France now preached a new crusade, producing an impression hardly less marvelous than Peter the Hermit had done half a century earlier. Among the immense concourse who listened to him were King Louis VII. of France and his wife, Queen Eleanor, surrounded by peers and prelates. While the hill-side was ringing with enthusiastic shouts of "God wills it!" Louis, throwing himself upon his knees, received the cross, and Eleanor immediately followed her husband's example. Such was then the demand from peasants, nobles, and bishops, that St. Bernard, finding the crosses for the occasion were insufficient, tore up his vestments to supply the demand.

By entering this crusade, Louis hoped to atone for the great sin of his life, which had so filled him with remorse that, for some time afterward, he had scarcely courage enough to look upon the light of day. When Louis had first taken up the reins of government he was obliged to lay siege to the insubordinate city of Vitey.

The inhabitants took refuge in a church. Louis caused it to be set on fire, and thus destroyed thirteen hundred people. The king was still brooding over this crime when news of the fall of Edessa reached France, and St. Bernard was commissioned by the pope to preach a new crusade.

Journey to the Holy Land.—After preaching throughout France, St. Bernard repaired to Germany. There he met with equal success, and Conrad the Third raised an army to accompany Louis.

In the spring of 1147 all Europe was stirring. Shepherds flung down their hooks, husbandmen abandoned their teams, traders quitted their booths, barons left their castles, bishops deserted their bishoprics to arm for the defense of the Holy Sepulcher. Queen Eleanor accompanied Louis, leading a body of women clad in knightly array. Conrad's army was followed by a similar band. Eleanor was attended by the troubadours of her court, that they might enliven the tedium of the expedition. (Read "Lay of Last Minstrel," by Scott; poetry and songs of troubadours and minstrels.)

Conrad's forces reached Constantinople first, but, perceiving the treacherous character of Emanuel, the grandson of Alexis, they continued their journey without waiting for the French. The perfidy of the Greeks now became manifest. Every city was fortified; every gate was closed. Provisions must be bought from the Greeks. The Greek guides kept the Saracens informed in regard to the Germans' line of march, and ambuscades awaited them at every defile. In the Taurus Mountains they were attacked by a Moslem army, who swept down upon them from the heights. Reduced to a tenth of their original number, they contrived to find their way back to Constantinople.

Louis's army met with like misfortunes, but a portion of it reached Antioch by embarking on vessels at Attalia. The French king and queen were warmly welcomed at Antioch, which was then under the government of Raymond of Poictiers, who had married the granddaughter of Bohemond of Tarentum. In this gay and brilliant court the Crusaders soon forgot the hardships they had endured and the comrades they had abandoned.

At length King Louis and Queen Eleanor, tearing themselves away from the pleasures of the court of Antioch, repaired to Jerusalem, whither Conrad had already gone in the guise of a pilgrim. Princes, prelates, and people sallied forth from the gates to meet him, and his arrival was hailed with loud shouts of "Blessed is he that cometh in the name of the Lord."

Attack on Damascus.—Baldwin the Third convoked a council at Acre to deliberate on the affairs of the kingdom. The assembly resolved to besiege Damascus. In June, 1149, a Christian army commanded by Conrad, the Emperor of Germany, and King Louis of France, marched to Damascus, and, taking possession of the gardens and orchards outside the city, commenced the siege. At first they carried all before them, but, when success seemed about to crown their efforts, a dispute arose between the Crusaders and the Syrian barons as to the possession of the city.

This discord finally caused them to abandon the enterprise in despair. Conrad and Louis were now both anxious to leave the East. The King of France, embarking at Acre, reached his capital in the autumn, with a mere fragment of his brilliant army. From this time Louis appeared more like a monk than a monarch, and Eleanor, indignant at the weakness he displayed, had her marriage dissolved. The divorced queen, still possessing the magnificent province of Aquitaine, had numerous suitors, one of whom was Henry Plantagenet of Normandy, an accomplished, handsome young man, heir to the throne of England. Eleanor married Henry, who soon became Henry II. of England. As queen of England she caused her husband much trouble by exciting her sons, Henry and Richard, to rebel against their father.—*Adapted from Edgar.*

THE THIRD CRUSADE.

The Three Leaders.—"The Third Crusade was caused by the capture of Jerusalem (1187) by Saladin, the Sultan of Egypt. Three of the great sovereigns of Europe, Frederick Barbarossa of Germany, Philip Augustus of France, and Richard I. of England, assumed the cross and set out, each at the head of a large army, for the recovery of the Holy City."—*Myers.*

Frederick Barbarossa was a grand-looking man, with fair hair and blue eyes, and a tinge of red in his beard, which made the Italians call him *Barbarossa*. He was unanimously chosen king by the German nobles and received his crown at Aix-la-Chapelle. Having established order in his own kingdom by punishing the robber-knights, and controlling the power of the dukes, he crossed the Alps into Italy, according to the custom of

German kaisars, to assert his rights there. It was a time of rival popes, and he entered into the controversy. The Italian cities, grown rich and powerful during the first crusades, appealed to him to settle their difficulties. He decided to punish the Milanese for their treatment of a rival city, by levelling their own city of Milan to the ground. All the neighboring cities, who were filled with deadly hatred toward this town, were allowed to exercise their vengeance upon it, and it was totally destroyed (1162). "The sacred relics in the churches were sent to enrich the churches of Germany. Among these were the reputed bodies of the Three Wise Men of the East, which were sent to Cologne, and are still exhibited there in the noted cathedral amid heaps of jewels." (See "Zigzag Journey of Northern Lands.")

When marching to Rome in midsummer, a terrible pestilence broke out in his army, compeling him to retreat with great loss to Germany. His rule in his own country was wise and vigorous. He founded Munich and several other great towns; but in the meantime the Italian cities had united with the pope against him, in what was called the Lombard League. Frederick crossed the mountains to put down this uprising, but the Lombards were stronger than he had expected, and in the midst of the struggle, at his greatest need, his vassal, the Duke of Saxony and Bavaria, refused his help, probably because he disliked fighting against the church. The Italians gained a complete victory. Frederick's horse was slain under him, and he was thought to be killed.

Frederick was forced to make peace (1176) and pay homage to the pope. The ceremony took place in St. Mark's Cathedral, Venice, at the door of which Alexander, the pope, awaited him with all the clergy. There the kaisar knelt to kiss the pope's slipper, and granted the freedom of the Italian cities. Frederick then retired to Germany, where he was all-powerful, and passed the evening of his life in peace and contentment.

On his return a great peace festival was held at Mentz, to which came forty thousand knights. "A camp of tents of silk and gold was set up by the Rhine, and musicians, called minne-singers, delighted the lords and ladies with songs of heroes and knights. The songs and ballads then sung became famous, and this festival may be said to be the beginning of musical art in music-loving Germany.

"Europe was now startled with the news that the Saracens, under Saladin, had taken Jerusalem. Barbarossa was about inaugurating a new war with the pope; but when this news came he and the pope became reconciled, and he resolved to go on a crusade.

"He was an old man now, but he entered into the crusade with the fiery spirit of youth. His war-cry was, 'Christ reigns! Christ conquers!'" Passing through Constantinople, he marched through Asia Minor, where he lost the flower of his army for want of food and water. He fought his way through every obstacle, and came without disaster to Iconium, where he gained a glorious victory over the sultan. Soon afterwards Barbarossa met his death in attempting to cross a swollen stream. "He was seventy years old when he was thus lost in the year 1190. His body was found and buried at Antioch."

The Germans could not believe their mighty kaisar was dead, but said that he had fallen a victim to enchantment. In the Kyffhauser cave, in Thuringia, he and his knights were thought to be sitting asleep around a stone table, his once red, but now white, beard growing through the stone. "They also said that the spell that bound Barbarossa and his knights would some day be broken, and that they would come back to Germany. This would occur when the country should be in sore distress, and need a champion for its cause.

"Ravens flew continually about the cave where the monarch and his knights were held enchanted. When they should cease to circle about it, the spell would be broken, and the grand old monarch would return to the Rhine.

"They looked for him in days of calamity; but centuries passed, and he did not return."—*Adapted from Miss Yonge and Butterworth.*

Richard the Lion Hearted (1189 to 1199).—"King Richard of England, surnamed Cœur de Leon, on account of his undaunted courage, is one of the favorite heroes of romance. He was tall and his figure extremely fine; he had a majestic and stately mien, and this, joined to his great courage and quickness of intellect, gave him on all occasions an ascendency over men's minds. But, though he possessed so many good qualities, he was hot-headed and without judgment.

"At his father's death in 1189, he expressed an agony of remorse for his undutiful conduct. One of the first acts of his reign was to release his mother from the long imprisonment enforced by King Henry.

"Being desirous of acquiring glory, Richard resolved to go on a crusade, for news had arrived that the Saracens had taken Jerusalem. [Saladin the Great; Frederick Barbarossa—See Edgar's "Crusades and Crusaders;" "Zigzag Journeys in Northern Lands."] His father had left him a large sum of money, but not enough for this purpose; so, in order to increase it, he sold the royal castle and estates, and also put to sale the offices of the greatest trust and power.

"When some of his ministers remonstrated with him on these proceedings, he said he would sell London itself, if he could find a purchaser. For a large sum of money, he absolved the King of Scotland from his vassalage to the King of England.

Richard and Philip at Sicily.—"At last his armament was ready, and Richard reached Messina, in Sicily, September, 1190. Here he was joined by Philip, King of France, and, as it was late in the season, they agreed to pass the winter in Sicily.

"There could scarcely be found two persons less alike in character than these two kings. Richard, though proud and domineering, was brave and generous. Philip was proud, but shy and deceitful. It is not surprising that two such opposite characters should quarrel before their six months' residence in Sicily was over. The cause of this disagreement was that Richard wished to break off his engagement with Philip's sister, to whom he had been betrothed in infancy, that he might marry Princess Berengaria of Navarre.

Richard's Marriage.—"Early in 1191, he prevailed upon his mother to bring the Princess Berengaria to Messina. They arrived the day before he had planned to sail for the Holy Land; but, as it was Lent, the marriage could not then be celebrated. Too enthusiastic to delay his enterprise for his wedding, he embarked in one galley and the princess, accompanied by the Queen of Sicily, Richard's sister, embarked in another for Acre. A violent storm arose, and the ship the two princesses were in, was in great danger. The King of Cyprus, however, refused to admit the vessel into his harbors, upon which Richard with his fleet laid siege to the island, and, soon taking possession of it, placed the king in silver chains. Richard remained on the island long enough to solemnize his marriage; then, leaving a governor to rule the island, he sailed for Acre. Here he found the King of France, who had left Sicily some time before, and was now awaiting his arrival before attacking Acre. Richard and his squadron of fifty war-galleys, thirteen store-ships, and more than a hundred transports were received with great enthusiasm.—*Goodrich*.

Description of Acre.—"Acre, situated on a promontory on the coast of Palestine, was in the eyes of the Crusaders one of the most important cities of the East. Surrounded on the land side by deep ditches, fortified with high walls and strong towers, and frequented by mariners and merchants from all parts of Europe and Asia, the capture and recovery of the place might well engage the attention of warriors."—*Edgar*. It had shared the fate of the other coast cities, as well as that of Jerusalem, when Saladin, the invincible warrior of the Mohammedans, proceeded from Egypt on his victorious career. It had been besieged for two years by a Christian army under the banner of Guy de Lusignan, who aspired to be king of Jerusalem. The Christians were now, in their turn, besieged by a large army of Saracens under the famous Saladin. When Philip arrived, he found the condition of the Christians in every way deplorable; "but the efforts he made to assist them in the attack were unsuccessful, and the courage of the Crusaders again dropped.

"The presence of the English might well revive the fainting courage of the Christians in the East. Cœur de Leon was considered a host in himself, and the men whom he led were proud of the prowess, and inspired by the spirit, of their king. Moreover, he was accompanied by Anglo-Norman nobles, who, as war-chiefs, had no rivals in Europe.

"But the grandeur of the English Crusaders tended to inspire hatred in the breasts of their rivals, and, in a few days discord appeared. Any feeling of friendship that existed between Richard and Philip had evaporated at Messina, and, within a week after their re-union, disputes about the disposal of the crown of Jerusalem revived their old feud. The two parties, ever ready to come to blows, were in no temper to unite their arms against the infidels. They were still contending when Cœur de Leon was prostrated with sickness."

Siege of Acre.—Philip vainly endeavored to reduce Acre without English aid. "Hoping to have the glory of accomplishing that in which his rival had failed,

Richard ordered his soldiers to prepare for an assault, and caused himself to be carried to the walls. The English advanced to the attack, the king appearing among them on a silken bed armed with an arbalist, from which he discharged arrows and darts at the besieged. Encouraged by inspiriting words and promises of reward, the English wrought deeds of valor; but the height of the walls and the courage of the Turks baffled all effort to take the city.

"Repeated failures convinced the kings of England and France of the impolicy of their conduct, and, harmony having been restored, they, in compact, besieged the city with great ardor. Many fierce and sanguinary conflicts took place between Saladin and the Crusaders, but neither side, for a time, gained any decided advantage. Nevertheless the Crusaders persevered with such effect that the besieged, suffering from famine and fatigue, proposed to capitulate."—*Edgar*.

The emirs consented to yield Acre, and to leave thousands as captives, on condition that the soldiers of the garrison were allowed to depart, unarmed. "Saladin on his part agreed to release all his Christian prisoners and to restore to the Crusaders the wood of the true cross, which he had taken in a former battle. But Saladin could not, or did not, at once comply with these conditions. The impetuous Richard would hear of no delay, and put to death all the Mohammedan prisoners, to the number of several thousand men. On account of this rashness and cruelty, Richard was justly charged with the death of as many Christian captives, whom Saladin slaughtered by way of reprisal.

Richard's Temper.—" Richard exhibited his violent temper upon another occasion. When the city of Acre surrendered, Leopold, Duke of Austria, caused his own banner to be displayed from the highest tower. Richard, highly exasperated at what he considered an insult, ordered the standard to be taken down, thrown into the ditch, and replaced by the banner of St. George. Leopold felt the indignity, but dissembled his anger and circumstances gave him the opportunity, as we shall soon relate, of taking an ample revenge, though at the expense of his faith and honor.

" The knightly qualities of Richard were more agreeable to the spirit of the age than the more statesmanlike ones of Philip. The rash valor and brilliant exploits in battle of the former gained him the applause of the multitude. Philip, who was of a jealous temperament, took offense at this, and his hatred for Richard was continually displaying itself.

Philip's Return.—" It was not long before Philip found out that nothing but barren laurels were to be gained in this war with the Saracens, and that but a small share of these would fall to his lot. He suddenly discovered that the air of Palestine was not favorable to his health. But before he went, he made a solemn promise not to make any attempts on the territories of Richard, though at this very time he entertained the full intention of attacking them as soon as he returned. Leaving his troops in Palestine, under the command of the Duke of Burgundy, he gave them secret orders to omit no opportunity of mortifying the English king."—*Goodrich.*

Journey Continued.—When Philip had sailed for Eu-

rope, King Richard gave orders that the whole army
should leave the captured city to continue their march
to Jerusalem. "Richard commenced his march along
the coast, having the sea on his right, and, on his left,
heights from which the Saracens watched his move-
ments, and awaited a favorable opportunity to attack
them. Day by day the great sultan infested the Crusaders' line of march, and, at the head of an army infinitely superior in numbers, caused them the utmost an-
noyance."—*Edgar*.

Battle of Assur.—While advancing toward the city of
Assur and entering a narrow plain, the Saracens offered
battle. "Part of the Moslem army covered the heights;
while the main body awaited the Crusaders on the margin of the river." Richard ordered his army to move
forward in a compact mass, without retaliating. The
Crusaders soon saw that they were surrounded on every
side, and at length, their plight became so intolerable that
the patience of the knights was rapidly giving away.
Murmurs were heard on every side, "but with a courage and calmness that would have done credit to Napo-
leon, he ordered his warriors to stand fast until the
Turks had emptied their quivers, and then to make the
charge. So, when Saladin's hosts had exhausted their
missiles upon the well-nigh impenetrable armor of the
Crusaders, Cœur de Leon advanced with the main army
of the Crusaders, and the shock was terrific. Fearful
was the revenge which those steel-clad warriors now
took upon the insolent foe. Christian and Moslem
fought hand-to-hand and steel-to-steel."—*Ridpath*. In
the midst of the battle, Richard, brandishing his axe,

and shouting, "St. George," was seen wherever the contest was the keenest. The very sight of that Cyprian steed, with its stalwart rider, was terrible to foes. "The bravest of Moslems watched with apprehension the Cyprian steed's furious rush; the bravest of Moslems recoiled in terror before the swing of Cœur de Leon's battle-axe. In vain, Saladin threw himself into the battle and crossed weapons with the mighty Plantagenet. Saracen after Saracen reeled to the ground, and it became impossible for them, notwithstanding their numbers, to withstand the onslaught of thousands of knights headed by such a hero-king. Broken and beaten on all sides, the Moslem warriors abandoned the field and retreated to the forest of oaks.

"The result of the battle mortified Saladin, and, calling together the emirs, he addressed them in anger.

"'Are these,' asked the sultan, 'the deeds of my brave troops, once so boastful, and whom I have so loaded with gifts? It is a disgrace to our nation, thus to become as nothing in comparison with their glorious ancestors.'

"'Most sacred sultan,' answered one of the emirs, 'this charge is unjust, for we fought with all our strength against the Franks, and did our best to destroy them. But it was of no avail, for they are encased in impenetrable armor, which no weapon can pierce. And further, there is among them one superior to any man we have ever seen. They call him Melech Ric, and he seems a king born to command the whole earth. He always charges before the rest, slaying our men; no man can resist him or escape out of his hands. What

more could we have done against a foe so formidable?'"
—*Edgar.*

Joppa.—After his great victory on the Assur, Richard led the pilgrim army to Joppa, which they found in a dilapidated condition. Cæsarea and Ascalon also fell into the hands of the Crusaders. It was the king's wish that they advance at once to Jerusalem, but the French barons insisted that the better policy was to tarry on the coast, rebuild the ruined fortresses and reserve the recapture of Jerusalem for the next campaign. Richard resolved to repair the ramparts of the cities, and worked like a private soldier to rebuild towers and clear out the moat. The work, however, was not to the liking of all, and he gave mortal offense by insisting that others should follow his example.

"I am neither carpenter nor mason," said Leopold, Duke of Austria, when pressed to leave the tent and take part in the operations.

"Many of the Crusaders, longing for scenes of revelry and dissipation, returned to gratify their tastes in the taverns of Acre."—*Adapted from Edgar.*

March Toward Jerusalem.—In the spring of 1192 the Crusaders once more rallied round the banner of Richard, eager to advance upon Jerusalem. All the knights took a solemn oath that they would not abandon the cause and the army proceeded from the coast as far as the valley of Hebron. Many Moslems fled from Jerusalem and Saladin himself gave up all for lost. Strange as it may appear, Richard stopped short in his victorious career when within sight of the Holy City. Was it the treachery of the Duke of Burgundy? Had Richard come to an understanding with Saladin or did he consider his resources insufficient for undertaking the siege of a city? Did the news from England, telling him of the intrigues of his treacherous brother, John, reverse his plans and destroy his hopes? None could answer.

Here in the valley of Hebron, with the towers of Jerusalem in view, the Lion Heart called a council, and it was decided that the present prosecution of the enterprise was inexpedient, and should be given up. It was not without pain that Richard gave the order to retreat. He covered his face with his hands and sadly turned away, declaring that he who could not redeem the Holy Sepulcher from the infidels was unworthy to behold it. —*Adapted from Ridpath.*

After this scene Richard fell back to Ascalon, and from thence to Acre. The French and Germans rapidly deserted his standard, and Saladin, descending from the mountains, took Joppa. On hearing that the citadel was still in the possession of the Crusaders, Richard at the head of his scanty ranks, went to their rescue. " He encountered an array of seven thousand on a plain outside the city of Joppa. Though infinitely inferior in number, Richard made a noble struggle, unhorsed every champion that crossed his path, spread consternation among his foes, and excited the admiration of his friends. Night put an end to the conflict, but Richard's victory was secure; and his marvelous feats of heroism filled the East with his fame. (Page 400, foot-note, Barnes; page 205, foot-note, Edgar).

"When winter came, Richard was eager to return to England. But the English king had no idea of stealing away as Philip Augustus had done. 'The sea is stormy,' he wrote to Saladin, ' yet if you are inclined to make peace, I will brave all its tempests and proceed to Europe; if you desire war, I will run all risks and besiege Jerusalem.'"—*Edgar.*

Truce.—A truce of three years and eight months was finally concluded between Richard and Saladin. It was agreed that the fortress of Ascalon should be dismantled as it was regarded a constant menace to Egypt. On the other hand, Tyre, Acre, and Joppa, with all the seacoasts between them, should remain to the Crusaders, and all Christian pilgrims who came unarmed should have free access to the holy places of Palestine, especially those in Jerusalem. "The king and sultan contended who should display most courtesy, and did not even require oaths to the terms, but contented themselves with their royal words, and touching the hands of each other's ambassadors. Christians and Moslems celebrated the conclusion of peace with tournaments and festivals, and most of the Crusaders, having visited the Holy City, embarked for Europe."—*Edgar.*

Richard's Return.—" Richard started on his homeward voyage in the autumn of 1192. After many storms at sea, Richard was at last shipwrecked on the coast of Dalmatia in the dominion of Leopold, the Duke of Austria, his old enemy. He now put on the disguise of a pilgrim, hoping to pass through Germany without being known. But the traveler displayed a generosity and profuseness more suitable to the king he was, than to the pilgrim he wished to appear.

" The intelligence soon spread through Germany, that

Hugh the Merchant was no other than Richard Plantagenet. The king arrived, however, without molestation at Saltzburg, and the governor there sent one of his knights to discover who he was. This man was by birth a Norman and instantly knew the king; but instead of betraying him, he presented him with a horse, and entreated him to fly and save himself. Accompanied by a boy and one other attendant, he reached a town near Vienna.

"Here he entered an inn, and, that no suspicion might be aroused concerning his rank, he busied himself turning the spit; but he forgot to conceal a splendid ring which he wore on his finger, and a man who had seen him at Acre, knew him and gave information to the Duke of Austria, who had not forgotten the insult offered to him after the capture of that city.

Captivity.—"The duke meanly seized the opportunity of vengeance which chance offered him, and threw the unfortunate prince into prison. His place of confinement was long kept concealed. There is a very pretty story told of the manner in which it was discoverd that is worth repeating:

"Blondel de Nesle, a favorite minstrel of Richard's, who had attended his person, devoted himself to discover his whereabouts. He wandered in vain from castle to palace, till he had heard that a strong fortress, on the banks of the Danube, was watched with peculiar strictness, as if containing some prisoner of distinction.

"The minstrel took his harp, and, approaching the castle as near as he durst, came so near the walls as to hear the captive soothing his imprisonment with music. Blondel touched his harp; the prisoner heard and was silent; upon this the minstrel played the first part of a tune, known to Richard, who instantly played the second part; and thus the faithful servant knew that the captive was no other than his royal master.

"This knowledge, however, was of little immediate advantage to Richard; for when the news reached the Emperor of Germany, he compelled the Duke to surrender his prisoner. The treatment of Richard was now worse than before; he was committed to a gloomy dungeon and loaded with chains."—*Goodrich.*

After a while he was taken to Worms, where a meeting of the princes of Germany, called a diet, was held. The Emperor, to justify his conduct, accused the English king of having driven Philip Augustus out of Palestine, and maltreated the Duke of Austria. He also accused him of treachery towards the interests and wishes of Christendom, the treaty with Saladin being wholly favorable to the Moslems. But Richard defended himself so eloquently and pathetically, that some of his judges shed tears on hearing him, and all were convinced of the malice of his accusers. Nevertheless, the spirit of the age permitted the Emperor to exact of his royal prisoner a ransom equal to about one and one-half million dollars.—*Adapted.*

Ransomed.—"Queen Eleanor, and everybody in England who loved King Richard—and there were many who did—used every means to raise the money required for his ransom. A general tax was levied to procure it, but, this not proving sufficient, the nobles voluntarily contributed a quarter of their yearly incomes, and the silver that was in the churches and monasteries was melted down.

"When the money was collected, Queen Eleanor took it herself to Germany, and had the happiness of receiving her son and bringing him to England. After an absence of four years he arrived at London in March, 1194, and was received with overflowings of joy."— *Goodrich.*

ENGLAND IN THE MIDDLE AGES.—*Continued.*

Richard, King of England.—"After Richard had settled the affairs of his kingdom, he set out for Normandy, to defend it from an attack with which it was threatened by Philip. One morning Prince John suddenly rushed into his apartment, and, throwing himself at his feet, implored his forgiveness. This the king immediately granted, though he could not feel any affection for such a brother. Indeed, he soon after said to some of his attendants, 'I wish I may forget my brother's injuries as soon as he will forget my pardon of them.'

"The remainder of Richard's life was passed in a succession of wars and truces with the King of France, who had neither the good faith to keep a treaty nor the courage to fight."

Richard Fatally Wounded.—In 1199, the Viscount of Limoges, a vassal of the king, had found a considerable treasure on his lands. Richard claimed this as his right as sovereign, but the viscount would yield only a part. Thereupon Plantagenet went with a band of warriors to take the castle of his refractory subject.

"The garrison offered to surrender the castle, and all that was in it, provided they might march out with their arms. Richard vindictively refused their offer, protesting he would take the place by force and put them all to death. As he was taking a survey of the castle and giving directions for the assault, he was wounded by an arrow from the bow of Bertram de Gourdon. The wound appeared trifling at first, but in a few days the life of the king was despaired of. Before he died the castle was taken, and all the garrison were instantly hanged, excepting Bertram, whom Richard ordered to be brought into his presence. 'What harm have I done you,' said the king to him, 'that you should thus have attempted my death?'

"'You have killed my father and brother with your own hands,' replied the man, 'and intended to have killed me, and I am ready to suffer with joy any torments you can invent, since I have been so lucky as to kill one who has brought so many miseries on mankind.' Richard, conscious of the truth of this bold reply, bore it with patience, and ordered the man to be set at liberty; but his command was not obeyed. Richard died on the 6th of April, 1199, in the forty-second year of his age, and tenth of his reign, only four months of which he had passed in England.."—*Goodrich*. (Character of Saladin—Read Scott's 'Talisman.')

King John and the Magna Charta.—King John, Richard's brother, was the worst king and the worst man that ever wore the crown of England. His nobles, tired out by his weakness and wickedness, drew up a declaration of rights. The king was called upon to sign this, but refused to do so. But being compelled to yield, he met the barons the 15th of June, 1215, in a large meadow near Windsor, called Runnymede, which means "the meadow of council," and was so called because it had been used by the Saxons for public meetings. At this meeting was signed the famous Magna Charta, which has since been considered as the foundation of English liberty.

By it the nobles were relieved from much of the oppressive tyranny of the feudal system. This had been constantly increasing, till no subject could act in the commonest affairs of life without the king's consent, which could be obtained only for money.

The great charter contains sixty-three articles, and yet only one of these is for the protection of the laboring people. It provides that even a farmer shall not, by any fine, be deprived of his carts, plows, and implements of husbandry.—*Adapted from Goodrich.*

The thirteenth century is also memorable for the formation of the House of Commons. The first regular English Parliament, composed of the two assemblies—the House of Lords and the House of Commons, was called (1265) in the reign of Henry III., son of John. Besides the barons, two knights from each county and two citizens from each city or borough represented the freeholders.

THE FOURTH CRUSADE.

The Fourth Crusade was a great piratical expedition and nothing else. It consisted of French and Germans under the leadership of the Count of Flanders. As it had been proved that the route by the sea was much to be preferred to that by land, the Crusaders went to Venice to demand ships.

Venice.—" Venice was then queen of the Adriatic. The inhabitants had been driven by Attila's invasion from the main land to the islands in the lagoons, and had found safety and prosperity in that situation, which is alone of its kind in the world. Not one of the ruling powers which had passed over Italy had been able to touch them. Their commerce was extensive; the islands of the Adriatic and the eastern coasts of the sea had recognized their supremacy. They seconded the crusades partly from religious conviction, and partly from a spirit of gain. The Mussulmans and the Greeks were their rivals in the eastern part of the Mediterranean. They considered it a good opportunity to dispossess them. Their services to the Crusaders procured for them in 1130 the privilege of exclusive quarters in each town of the new kingdom of Jerusalem. At the same time they took possession of the Greek islands of Rhodes, Samos, Scio, Lesbos, and Andros. In Venice the reconciliation took place between Frederick Barbarossa and the pope, which restored peace to Italy. A slab of red porphyry still marks the place in the vestibule of St. Mark, where the interview occurred. In memory of that event and of the Venetian victory on the Adriatic, the pope gave the chief of Venice that ring which the doge or ruler of Venice threw into the sea as a token of marriage with the Adriatic. After that, this ceremony was repeated every year, with a pomp that exalted the pride and patriotism of the Venetians. The government of Venice was aristocratic and the office of doge was elective."—*Duruy*.

Such was Venice when the ambassadors of the Crusaders arrived. The veteran doge of Venice, Henrico Dandolo, now ninety-three years of age and blind as a stone, but still fired with the zeal and spirit of youth, convened the councils of state, and afterward called together the citizens in the great square of St. Mark. "Here in the presence of the assembled state of Venice the French barons knelt before the majesty of the people, and besought, with all the fervor of eloquence, the aid of the republic in the recovery of the holy places of the East."—*Adapted from Ridpath*.

In return for so great a service the mercantile city of Venice could not do otherwise than make it a matter of business. They agreed to furnish a fleet of fifty galleys, four thousand knights, nine thousand men-at-arms, and twenty thousand infantry with horse and accoutrements, and provisions for nine months—all for the sum of eighty-five thousand marks or more than $800,000.—*Compiled from Duruy*.

The Crusaders could not raise such a large sum of money. After more than a year's time only fifty thousand marks were secured. The doge and citizens of the Republic refused to permit the departure of the fleet until the entire amount should be paid.

At length the doge proposed that instead of the present payment of the remaining marks, the Crusaders should assist him in reducing the revolted city of Zara on the coast of Dalmatia. The remaining indebtedness might then be paid at the close of the Crusade. He also promised, if this proposition met their approval, to assume the cross himself and conduct the fleet against the Syrian infidels.

In spite of the anathemas of the pope, the Crusaders and Venetians, under the command of the blind old doge, in 1202, besieged Zara and took possession of it after five days' siege. The lives of the inhabitants were spared, but the fortifications were torn down and the city itself given up to pillage.

In the following year the Crusaders and Venetians, entirely turned from their original purpose, laid siege to Constantinople. They stormed the city, plundered its palaces, and destroyed its precious monuments. A Latin Empire was now established at Constantinople. This lasted half a century, but was broken up by the Greeks in 1261, when the Byzantine capital again became a Greek city.—*Complied from Edgar.* (Invasion of Tartars, page 282, Duruy; Children's Crusade; Gray, and "Zigzag Journeys in Classic Lands.")

THE LAST CRUSADER.

King Edward I of England became leader of the Seventh Crusade on the death of St. Louis, in 1270. He gathered a formidable force, with which he landed at Acre, then held by the Christians. The movement was futile in recovering more of the Holy Land, and he soon returned home. Edward is known in history as the "Last of the Crusaders."

Left to the Savior's conquering foes,
The land that girds the Savior's grave;
Where Godfrey's crozier-standard rose,
He saw the crescent banner wave.
There, o'er the gently broken vale,
The halo light on Zion glowed;
There Kedron, with a voice of wail,
By tombs of saints and heroes flowed;
There still the olives silver o'er
The dimness of the distant hill;
There still the flowers that Sharon bore
Calm air with many an odor fill.
Slowly the Last Crusader eyed
The towers, the mount, the stream, the plain,
And thought of those whose blood had dyed
The earth with crimson streams in vain!
He thought of that sublime array—
The hosts that over land and deep
The Hermit marshaled on their way,
To see those towers and halt to weep.
Resigned the loved, familiar lands,
O'er burning wastes the cross to bear,
And rescue from the Paynim's hands
No empire save a sepulcher!
And vain the hope, and vain the loss,
And vain the famine and the strife;
In vain the faith that bore the cross,
The valor prodigal of life!
And vain was Richard's lion-soul,
And guileless Godfrey's patient mind,
Like waves on shore, they reached the goal,
To die and leave no trace behind!
"O God!" the last Crusader cried.
"And art Thou careless of Thine own?
For us Thy Son in Salem died,
And Salem is the scoffer's throne!
And shall we leave, from age to age,
To godless hands the Holy Tomb?
Against Thy saints the heathen rage—
Launch forth Thy lightnings, and consume!"

> A form flashed, white-robbed, from above;
> All Heaven was in those looks of light,
> But Heaven, whose native air is love.
> "Alas!" the solemn vision said,
> "Thy god is of the shield and spear—
> To bless the quick and raise the dead,
> The Savior God descended here!
> Ah! know'st thou not the very name
> Of Salem bids thy carnage cease,—
> A symbol in itself to claim
> God's people to a Home of Peace?
> Ask not the Father to reward
> The hearts that seek, through blood, the Son;
> O Warrior, never by the sword
> The Savior's Holy Land is won."
> —*Sir E. Bulwer-Lytton.*

Results of the Crusades.—Asia apparently triumphed. Palestine remained in the hands of the Mohammedans after they had completely conquered it in 1291. Though the Crusades had failed of their direct object, they had produced marked results both good and evil.—*Adapted.*

"Among their advantages, it may be observed that they had a refining influence on the ruder nations of the North, by bringing them in contact with Constantinople and the rich cities of Italy, then the centers of Christian civilization and art. They diffused a knowledge of useful inventions and arts, in which the Orientals were then proficient. They promoted commerce, and eventually revived an interest in manufactures." "New industries were brought back from the East; the tissues of Damascus, which were imitated at Parma and Milan; glass from Tyre, which was copied at Venice, where looking-glasses were made to replace the metal mirrors; the use of wind-mills, of flax, of silk, of a number of useful plants, such as the Damascus plum tree, the sugar cane, which was to supersede honey, the only sugar known to antiquity, but which at first could only be cultivated in Sicily or Spain, whence it passed later to Madeira and the Antilles, bringing great wealth with it; and, finally, the mulberry tree, which first enriched Italy, then France. Cotton fabrics began to be known during this epoch, though no cotton industry of any importance was founded in France before the seventeenth century. Paper made from cotton had been known for a long time; linen paper was known by the end of the thirteenth century, but it did not entirely replace parchment until the sixteenth century. Damaskening and the engraving of seals and coins were being perfected. The art of enameling was learned, and the goldsmith's art received a new impulse."—*Duruy and Quackenbos.*

" On the other hand, the Crusade cost Europe two millions of efficient men and vast amounts of treasure; they unsettled sober industries, encouraged profligacy, and for a time rolled back the tide of order and civilization which had set in after the inundations of the Norsemen.

" Whatever the effect, whether good or bad, on the general condition of the people, there is no doubt that the Crusades contributed to the overthrow of feudalism and the strengthening of the power of the church. To raise means for the equipment of their forces, the nobles in many cases were obliged to part with their fiefs. Numbers fell in battle, and left their lands to the crown or to the church. Cities, in return for advances of money. obtained an increase of privileges, and thus the power of knights and nobles, as a class, diminished, while that of the kings, the church, and the cities, proportionately increased.

"A better knowledge of geography, which had before been imperfect, was one of the results of the travel and adventure in the East. Such stories as were told in a geographical work of the eleventh century, that the inhabitants of Russia had but one leg and one eye, were no longer currently believed. In fact, a spur was given to exploration, which subsequently led to the doubling of the Cape of Good Hope and the discovery of America."—*Quackenbos*. (Read story of Marco Polo.)

The Growth of the Cities.—"We have already mentioned in connection with the castles, the settlements which grew up beneath the shadow of their walls. It was to the interest of the lord of the castle to enlarge these communities, thereby increasing the number of his subjects and artisans and augmenting his revenues, and even his military forces; for many a time the men, whether from the towns or from villages, were seen marching, led by their priest, wherever their lord directed. He also tried to attract the peasants from the neighboring domains by the advantages he offered on his land."

In all the cities a middle class was formed which grew richer day by day through commerce and industry. They filled the universities, and acquired knowledge, especially legal knowledge. In England the towns united with the nobility against the power of royalty; in Germany, as in France, they allied themselves with the sovereign against the feudal system. The serfs of the neighboring lords took refuge in the cities, and at the end of a year and a day they could not be redeemed." This gave rise to many complaints on the part of the lords and caused almost perpetual war between the cities and the nobles. The cities were thus compelled to unite for mutual protection and became more and more a power in the land.

"The towns in *Germany* which enjoyed the greatest prosperity were those lying on the Rhine and in Lorraine; Mainz, Cologne, Coblenz, Bonn, Aix-la-Chapelle; in Saxony, Magdeburg, Bremen, and Hamburg; in Franconia, Frankfort on the Main, Spire, Worms, etc. Their commerce extended far and wide; they exchanged commodities from the north of Europe for those of the East."

Hanseatic League.—"In the low countries of the north of Germany and France, which were often flooded by water and intersected by rivers, the cities naturally were stronger than the feudal nobility. From their situation on the ocean and at the mouth of great rivers, which could carry their ships in all directions into the very heart of a vast continent, they naturally devoted themselves to commerce; but with this difference from the Italian cities, that, whereas the latter always looked upon each other as rivals, as there was no powerful feudal system in their midst to force them to unite against a common foe, the German cities formed a confederation in the interest of mutual protection. This confederation, called the Hanseatic League, held the supreme power in the north of Europe, and united all the cities of the Baltic, the Rhine, and the great communes of Flanders.

"From London to Novgorod, on all the vessels of commerce and above all the counting-houses, floated one and the same flag—that of the Hansa. The merchants of this league were masters of the fisheries, the mines, the agriculture, and the manufactures of Germany. In their markets were exchanged the furs, tallow, and hides from Russia; grain, wax, and honey from Poland; amber from Prussia; metals from Saxony and Bohemia; wines from the Rhine and France; wool and tin from England; linens from Holland and Friesland; cloths from Flanders; and, last but not least, the Italians and Provencals sent the products of the Orient to the great free port of Bruges. In 1360, there were fifty-two cities in this confederation, and in the eighteenth century eighty cities." (Poem "Ghent," "Antwerp," "Bruges." See Longfellow's and Ford's Historical Poems.)

Flanders.—"Flanders, situated in the very midst of this great commercial association of Germany, and covered with cities and workshops, was a zealous center of industry. Ghent numbered 80,000 citizens able to bear arms; Ypres counted 200,000 weavers within her walls and suburbs; Bruges, the entrepot of all Flanders, was the meeting-place of European merchants. The whole world was clothed in English wool, which had been manufactured in Flanders. All the kingdoms of Christendom, and even the Turks, were disturbed by the war that broke out between the cities and the count in 1380.

Amsterdam, Holland.—"In the thirteenth century, an

inundation of the ocean joined the Zuyder Zee with the ocean, and made Amsterdam a port secure from all tempests; in the fourteenth century, the change of the herring fishery, which left the shores of Scania for the shores of England and Holland, brought a great source of wealth to these countries."—*Duruy*. (Read "Hans Brinker.")

HOLLAND.

Where the Rhine,
Branched out in many a long canal, extends,
From every province swarming, void of care,
Batavia rushes forth; and, as they sweep,
On sounding skates, a thousand different ways,
In circling poise, swift as the winds, along,
The then gay land is maddened all to joy.
—*James Thomson*.

HOLLAND.

To men of other minds my fancy flies,
Embosomed in the deep where Holland lies.
Methinks her patient sons before me stand,
Where the broad ocean leans against the land,
And, sedulous to stop the coming tide,
Lift the tall rampire's artificial pride.
Onward, methinks, and diligently slow,
The firm, connected bulwark seems to grow;
Spreads its long arms amidst the watery roar,
Scoops out an empire, and usurps the shore;
While the pent ocean, rising o'er the pile,
Sees an amphibious world beneath him smile:
The slow canal, the yellow-blossomed vale,
The willow-tufted bank, the gliding sail,
The crowded mart, the cultivated plain,
A new creation rescued from his reign.
—*Oliver Goldsmith*.

THE STORKS.

Where the Rhine loses his majestic force
In Belgian plains, won from the raging deep
By diligence amazing, and the strong,
Unconquerable hand of Liberty,
The stork-assembly meets; for many a day,
Consulting deep and various ere they take
Their arduous voyage through the liquid sky;
And now their route designed, their leaders chose,
Their tribes adjusted, cleaned their vigorous wings;
And many a circle, many a short essay,
Wheeled round and round, in congregation full
The figured flight ascends; and, riding high
The aerial billows, mixes with the clouds.
—*James Thomson.*

(Read other poems—"The Leak in the Dike," by Phœbe Carey; "Holland in the Olden Time," by John Bowring. See Longfellow's " Poems of Europe.")

England.—" Under King John, the granting of charters became a frequent occurrence. From that time on, the cities, grown rich and powerful, inspired respect in their lords, whether kings or barons, who no longer exacted but asked the cities and towns of their domains for assistance; the foremost citizens of London, Dover, Sandwich and Hastings even acquired the title of nobles and barons. In 1264 the above mentioned towns, together with York and Lincoln and all the other great cities of England were authorized to send deputies to parliament. This marks their first appearance in political life. One hundred and twenty towns sent deputies to the parliament convoked by Edward in 1295."

" In England, both commerce and industry were still dormant. Nevertheless, England had some commercial relations with Spain, from which she received Arab horses in exchange for her fine sheep. The best English herds of to-day are descended from the Arab horses."— *Duruy*. (Poem, " Homes of England," by Mrs. Hemans; poem, " Rule Britannia," by James Thomson.)

THE HOMES OF ENGLAND.

The stately homes of England,
  How beautiful they stand,
Amidst their tall ancestral trees,
  O'er all the pleasant land!
The deer across their greensward bound
  Through shade and sunny gleam,
And the swan glides past them with the sound
  Of some rejoicing stream.

The merry homes of England
  Around their hearths by night,
What gladsome looks of household love
  Meet in the ruddy light!
There woman's voice flows forth in song,
  Or childhood's tale is told;
Or lips move tunefully along
  Some glorious page of old.

The blessed homes of England,
  How softly on their bowers,
Is laid the holy quietness
  That breathes from Sabbath hours!
Solemn, yet sweet, the church bells' chime
  Floats through their woods at morn,
All other sounds in that still time
  Of breeze and leaf are born.

The cottage homes of England
  By thousands on her plains,
They are smiling o'er the silvery brooks,
  And round the hamlet fanes.
Through glowing orchards forth they peep,
  Each from its nook of leaves,
And fearless there the lowly sleep
  As the bird beneath their eaves.

> The free, fair homes of England,
> Long, long, in hut and hall,
> Many hearts of native proof be reared
> To guard each hallowed wall.
> And green forever be the groves,
> And bright the flowery sod,
> Where first the child's glad spirit loves
> Its country and its God.
>
> —*Mrs. Hemans.*

Mediterranean Cities.—"The commerce on the Mediterranean flourished long before that of the North. Without mentioning the cities on the African coast which were so prosperous during the tenth and eleventh centuries, or the Arabs in Spain, who were so industrious and so rich, there were Barcelona, the store-house and market of Spain, Montpellier, Narbonne, Marseilles, Nice, Genoa, Pisa, Florence, Amalfi, and Venice, which were all struggling for the supremacy over the eastern commerce. The Italian cities gained the greater part, and scattered their counting-houses over the coasts of the Archipelago and the Black Sea, where Venice and Genoa ruled, either simultaneously or by turns."

Intermediate Stations.—Intermediate stations between the Mediterranean cities and those of the North and Baltic Seas became necessary. Marseilles, Beaucaire, Lyons, and Troyes served France; Constance, Basle, and Strassburg for the Rhine country; Innsbruck for the Alps; Augsburg for the great Bavarian plain; Ulm, Ratisbon, and Vienna for the Danube, and Nuremberg for Franconia. In these cities, the products of the North and South were exchanged.—*Adapted.*

France.—"In France, in the twelfth century, annual

fairs, which were famous throughout Europe, were held at Troyes in Champagne, Beaucaire, and St. Denis, near Paris. The merchants of Rouen, Orleans, Amiens, and Rheims kept up relations with the rich factories of Flanders and the immense warehouses of Bruges. Those of Lyons, Nimes, Avignon, and Marseilles went twice a year to Alexandria in search of the commodities of the East, which reached France also through Venice and the German cities. Bordeaux already exported wines to England and Flanders. The cities of Languedoc bought fine weapons at Toledo, and the hangings of leather worked with arabesques at Cordova. Paris had an association for the merchandise which came by water. Hence the vessel which is still to be seen on the shield of the city. Saint Louis took the merchants under his special protection."—*Duruy.*

IV. SWITZERLAND.

In the time of the Romans, Switzerland was called Helvetia. It was subject to the Franks in the sixth century. After the division of Charlemagne's empire the northern part had become incorporated in the German Empire; but the ancient forest cantons on Lake Lucerne had never been conquered and were only under the protection of the emperors.

"In the twelfth century the cities—Zurich, Basle, Berne and Freiberg—began to be centers of trade, and gained municipal privileges."

For some time after the beginning of the thirteenth century the German emperors proved lenient masters. In 1298, however, Albert I, styled Duke of Austria, "proposed to unite the free Swiss towns to his Austrian estates, and this occasioned a memorable struggle for liberty. Albert appointed as governor an unscrupulous tyrant, Gessler, whose acts of oppression aroused the slumbering spirit of the Swiss. According to legendary history the hero *William Tell* was the liberator of his country. Refusing to bow before the ducal cap of Austria, which Gessler had elevated on a pole in the market-place of Altorf, Tell was seized and condemned by the governor to pierce with an arrow an apple placed on the head of his son." (See Knowles' poem of "William Tell" in "McGuffey's Fifth Reader"; also the sonnet "William Tell" by W. C. Bryant.)

"In 1386 a small force of Swiss gained another great victory over the Austrians at Sempach. In this battle *Arnold Winkelried* cried to his countrymen: "Dear brothers, I will open a way for you; take care of my wife and children." Then, rushing on the bristling spears of the Austrians, he gathered as many as he could within his grasp, and thus opened a path for his comrades into the ranks of the foe. (See poem in "Indiana Fifth Reader.")

"The independence of Switzerland was not fully established till the end of the fifteenth century."— *Quackenbos*. (See story of John Huss in histories.)

ENGLAND IN MIDDLE AGES (CONCLUDED.)

The First Prince of Wales (1283).—Wales and Ireland had both been reduced to submission in the twelfth century by Henry II, father of Richard the Lion-hearted.

In the thirteenth century, Llewellyn, the Welsh chief, declined to go to London to serve the new king, Edward I., grandson of John. A military expedition was at once sent to subdue the country. Inspired by the wild poetry of their bards, the Welsh gallantly defended their liberties; but Llewellyn was eventually slain (1282), and King Edward, in order to conciliate the people, promised them a native-born sovereign who could speak no English. When their barons assembled, he presented them his own son Edward, born a few days before in the Welsh castle of Carnarvon, and the chieftains kissed the hands of the *first Prince of Wales*.

War With Scotland.—"The ambition of Edward I. led him to attempt the annexation of Scotland. He at first proposed the marriage of the Scottish princess to his son, thinking by this means to consolidate the whole island into one monarchy. The plan was favorably received, but unfortunately frustrated by the decease of the Scottish child-queen. Thirteen nobles at once claimed the vacant throne, chief of whom were *John Baliol* and *Robert Bruce*. The Scots asked Edward to decide the question of succession." He decided in favor of Baliol, on condition of his doing homage to the English monarch as his feudal lord. The Scots, impatient of their vassalage, soon revolted. Baliol renounced his allegiance but was captured by Edward and incarcerated in the Tower of London.

"Scotland, however, was still unsubdued; a temporary deliverer appeared in the person of *Sir William Wallace*, against whom a powerful English army was promptly dispatched. Its commander, finding the Scots strongly posted on the Forth, sent two friars to propose a truce. 'Go tell your masters,' said Wallace, 'we came not here to treat, but to set Scotland free.' Enraged at this defiance, the English advanced and began to cross the river on a narrow bridge. When half the force had made the passage the Scots fell upon it and gained a complete victory.

"For a time *Wallace* acted as 'Guardian of the Realm,' but at last, defeated and betrayed by a follower to Edward, he was condemned as a traitor, and dragged at the tails of horses to the scaffold. His head, crowned in mockery with a wreath of laurel, was set on London Bridge.

"*Robert Bruce*, grandson of the rival of Baliol, next arose as the restorer of his country's liberties, and after gaining some advantages over the English, was crowned king (1306). Edward, now an old man, again set out to conquer Scotland, but was overtaken on the way by death. He made his son promise to continue the war against the Scots, carrying his bones at the head of the army, for he believed that even the presence of these would be sufficient to insure victory.

"*Edward II.* failed to comply with the dying injunction of his father, and led his army back into England. He buried the dead monarch at Westminster with this inscription on his tomb, 'Edward I., the Hammer of the Scotch.'"

"Edward had spent his youth in the society of dissolute companions, and now, surrounded by unworthy favorites, he gave himself up to dissipation. Bruce, meanwhile, with a little band, bravely struggled in the cause of his country; now foiling the blood-hounds that bayed on his track, now holding the mountain-pass single-handed against a host of foes. After many hair-breadth escapes, fortune rewarded his efforts, and nearly all Scotland was recovered from the English.

Bannockburn (1314).—These successes finally awakened Edward from his indifference. He took the field at the head of a large army, and came up with Bruce on the *burn*, or *brook*, of *Bannock*. The evening before the battle an English knight, perceiving Bruce riding in front of his army on a small Highland pony, bore down upon him with his lance. But the Scot parried the thrust, and, rising in his stirrups, cleft his adversary's skull to the chin with one stroke of his battle-axe. This feat was looked upon as a good omen by his followers. In the gray of the morning they were led to the field by an abbot, barefoot and with a crucifix in his hand. The English, seeing them kneel as he prayed, shouted, 'They beg for mercy!' 'Yes,' said the knight, 'but only from God.'

"The Scotch force was protected in front by pits filled with sharp stakes and concealed by sods; hence, when the English charged, their horses were entangled and the riders thrown. Bruce won the day, and Edward fled from the kingdom, pursued by the Scottish cavalry.

"The victory of Bannockburn naturally secured the independence of Scotland." By the accession of James VI. of Scotland to the English throne in 1603, England and Scotland were united under one sovereign.—*Quackenbos*. (Read "Scottish Chiefs," by Jane Porter, and

"Days of Bruce," by Grace Aquilar; also stories of Robert Bruce in readers.)

Hundred Years' War.—From the time of William the Conqueror the English kings had laid claim to territory in France. This claim was increased by the marriage of Eleanor of Aquitaine and Henry Plantagenet. In 1328, Edward III. of England declared himself to be the nearest male heir to the throne of France, and commenced his preparations for an invasion to assert his rights. A long and wasteful war between England and France called the *Hundred Years' War* was the result. Like the Peloponnesian War of Ancient Greece it was not one continuous struggle, but was broken by occasional truces, owing to the exhaustion of the contesting parties.—*Adapted*. *Battle of Cre'cy*. Landing at Normandy (1346) Edward encountered Philip of France on the plain of Cre'cy. In this memorable battle the English yeomanry were more than a match for the chivalry of France.

"The French peasant at that time was a poor miserable serf who had never handled arms. In England there were farmers and stout peasants who used to practice shooting with the bow once a week." The French having no footmen to meet these sturdy English archers hired a body of Genoese cross-bow men to lead the advance. Just before the battle a shower of rain fell which slackened the bow-strings of the Genoese archers; but the English had their bows safe in leathern cases and their strings were in full order. The arrows galled the French Knights so that a charge was ordered to cut the English archers down. But full in the way stood the poor Genoese fumbling to tighten their strings; and the knights, becoming impatient at the delay, cut them down right and left, thus spending their strength against their own army. It was no wonder that the French were defeated with the loss of thirty thousand soldiers and twelve hundred knights—the flower of their chivalry.— *Adapted from Miss Yonge.*

"Edward's eldest son, then only sixteen years old, called the *Black Prince*, from the color of his armor, commanded a division of the English. He was at one time almost overwhelmed by the foe, but his father refused to send him aid, in order that the boy might 'win his spurs.'"—*Quackenbos.* The honor of knighthood had been conferred on him by Edward just before the battle, and the Black Prince proved worthy of the confidence. (See story of Black Prince in Goodrich's English History.)

"It is said that the front of Edward's army was protected by some pieces of *cannon*, the *first* that had yet been made use of in any battle in Europe. These cannons were very clumsy machines. They were composed of bars of iron, held together by hoops, and they commonly burst at the third or fourth discharge. They were at first employed to shoot off darts and arrows."— *Goodrich.*

The result of the victory at the battle of Cre'cy was the capture of Calais by the English. For two hundred years this seaport afforded a convenient landing-place for the invasion of France.

The English continued to gain advantage until in 1420 the French had become so discouraged that a large party agreed that the crown of France should be given to Henry V. upon the death of Charles VI., the crazy king of France. Both kings died, however, within two months of each other.

Siege of Orleans.—"The infant son of Henry V. of England was now proclaimed king of England and France, and his uncle, the Duke of Bedford, who had been appointed protector, took the field to maintain his cause. The true heir to the French monarchy was the Dauphin, Charles VII., who was supported principally in the southern provinces. The English gained ground, and at last laid siege to Orleans, the most important city in the possession of Charles. After a severe blockade the town was on the eve of capitulating, when a poor peasant-girl appeared on the stage to rescue France, in the summer of 1425."—*Quackenbos.*

Joan of Arc, the Maid of Orleans.—"Far away among the hills of Lorraine, in the eastern part of France, lived Joan of Arc, the daughter of a cottager, whose flock she tended. In her hours of solitude she saw visions, and said that voices called to her from the woods. There was an old tradition that a girl from the forests of Lorraine would one day save France, and when she heard of the disasters that were befalling her country, Joan felt herself impelled to offer her services to the Dauphin, assured that the tradition would find its fulfillment.

"Having proved her power to the king's satisfaction, by singling him out, though disguised, from a hundred knights who were present, Joan was sent to the army. She appeared in camp clad in a suit of white armor and mounted on a war horse; her head was unhelmeted and her long black hair fell down around her shoulders. The rough men-at-arms received her with enthusiasm, and at her bidding left off their profanity and evil habits. She marched at their head, displaying a consecrated banner, and effected an entrance into Orleans with a supply of provisions for the famishing citizens. From this moment success deserted the standard of the English; their forts fell into the hands of Joan, and the siege was soon raised. From her heroism in relieving the beleaguered city, Joan was called the 'Maid of Orleans.'

"Charles was subsequently crowned at Rheims, while the Maid stood by his side in complete armor. Having now performed her double mission, she knelt at his feet and prayed for her discharge. But Charles induced her to remain,—and for a sad fate. She was taken prisoner by the English, condemned for witchcraft and burned at the stake. The ungrateful king offered no ransom, proposed no exchange for the maid who had saved his crown. His end was almost as terrible as hers; he starved himself to death from the dread of being poisoned by his son, afterward Louis XI.

"The English profited little by the execution of Joan. 'We are lost' was the prediction of one of their own number who witnessed her death, 'we have burned a saint.' One by one their conquests were forced from them; and, when the Hundred Years' War ended in 1451, Calais alone remained in their possession."—*Quackenbos*. (Read Miss Kirkland's " Hist. of France" and " Hist. of England.")

FALL OF THE GREEK EMPIRE (1453).

"The last great event of the Middle Ages was the extinction of the Eastern Empire by the capture of Constantinople." The empire had been reduced to a state of debility before the Crusades. After the Venetians were driven out in 1261, it was equally exposed to the depredations of the Christians and the Turks, preserving only a high-sounding name, while it stood on the brink of destruction. "Narrow, superstitious ideas directed the measures of government, while they did not check the course of heinous crimes." "One of the feeble monarchs of Constantinople suffered himself to be persuaded that the Greek Empire was under the peculiar protection of Heaven, and, therefore, a fleet was unnecessary for its defense." "For this reason, the country was ravaged by pirates, and then overrun by the Ottoman Turks, so-called from their leader, Othman."—*Compiled from Goodrich.* (Page 493, Duruy.)

Soliman.—These Turks, from the opposite bank, saw the splendor of the many towns ruled by the cross, and their eyes continually brooded upon the great rich city of Constantinople. One night Soliman, the grandson of Othman, was seated in the midst of the ruins of a conquered city, watching by the light of the moon the sparkling waters of the Sea of Marmora, which led to the object of their great desire. "It seemed to him that the shadows thrown by the colossal ruins of the destroyed city lengthened out before him like a bridge across the sea, and at the same time mysterious voices reminded him that the empire of the world had been promised to his race. 'This is a sign of God,' he said. When day broke, he caused two rafts to be built, on which he embarked with thirty-nine men. One of the Greek emperors had recently asked his assistance in opposing a rival, and Soliman, at the head of 10,000 horsemen, had gone all through Thrace and Bulgaria, ravaging as he went. On his return he noticed how poorly guarded were the Greek fortresses on the straits. He surprised one of them with his thirty-nine men. Shortly after, an earthquake put into his hands the best fortification of the region—Gallipoli—whence the frightened inhabitants made their escape, flying what they believed to be the wrath of Heaven. The wrath of Heaven did indeed visit their city, but it came in the guise of the Turks. From that day they had gained a footing in Europe (1356).''—*Duruy*.

Janizaries.—The Sultan Amurath, son of Soliman, organized the Turkish infantry, called Janizaries (new soldiers). This formidable body was made up of the stoutest and handsomest of the captive youth selected annually for service in the army. "Educated to the religion of their masters, and trained in arms, they formed, like the Prætorian Guard of Rome, a powerful bodyguard that was a terror to Europe."

Capture of Adrianople.—Soliman had opened the gates of Europe to the Turks. Under Amurath they rushed in, but before they attacked Constantinople directly, they turned to her surroundings. Amurath took Adrianople (1360) and made it his residence. "When he pitched his tent in the midst of implacable enemies he made it necessary for the existence of his people that they should continue the conquest of the country, and by taking his stand in the second town of importance in Thrace, he forced them sooner or later to capture the first in rank."—*Duruy*.

John Paleologus.—The emperor of Constantinople, to avert the danger, went himself to Rome to bring about the union of the Greek and Roman churches. The unfortunate monarch exhausted his last resources upon his journey, and when, nothing being accomplished, he tried to return to the East, he was retained by his creditors. His son, Manuel, was obliged to sell all he possessed to gain the release of his father. The emperor then decided to pay tribute to the sultan, to become his vassal and follow him in his wars. The conquering Turks penetrated as far as the Save, and entered Thessaly and then Morea. Fear of them spread in the mountains of Austria and beyond the Adriatic.

" While the Turks were gaining these victories, Constantinople lived in constant fear, and tried to avert the wrath of the sultan by abject submission. John Paleologus paid the sultan a tribute of 30,000 gold crowns, and with a body of twelve thousand men assisted him in conquering the Greek towns of Asia Minor. In 1391, he built two towers near one of the city gates. The sultan ordered him to demolish them, if he did not wish his son Manuel, who was then in his service, to have his eyes put out. He obeyed. This same Manuel, when his father died, escaped from the court of the sultan, and returned to Constantinople. The sultan immediately blockaded the city for seven years, until the Turks were allowed to have a mosque and a cadi (judge) in the very city. In

1400, Manuel went to Paris and London displaying all the miseries of the great title he bore, and besought aid against the Turks. He even begged money to support his life, and he counted himself happy to obtain a pension of 30,000 crowns from France. The last moment of the Greek Empire seemed to have come, when more efficient help arrived from an unsuspected quarter."

Tamerlane.—Another Mongol invasion occurred under Tamerlane, a descendant of Genghis Kahn. Like his ancestor, he attempted to extend his empire from the Pacific to the banks of the Vistula and Danube. He conquered Great Tartary, Persia, and invaded India. At Ispahan he put 70,000 persons to death; in Khorassan, he had already massacred the whole population, except 2,000 men, who were later piled one upon the other, with mortar and brick to serve as foundation for several towers which he wished to build. Later, before he arrived at Delhi, India, being embarrassed by the existence of 100,000 captives, he had them put to death. He amused himself in building at the city gates, pyramids of twenty or thirty thousand heads. Attila and his Huns were left far behind. In Russia, after making a victorious passage as far as the neighborhood of Moscow, a lack of forage and the severity of the climate forced him to retreat (1393). In 1398 he was to be found at the other extremity of his empire and of Asia. He was then sixty-two years old; neither age nor fatigue had any power over him; he dreamed of the conquest of the Indies. "His tired emirs asked for rest; he read them the Koran, which imposes an eternal combat with idolators." He spread terror upon the banks of the Indus and Ganges; from there through southwestern Asia, burning Aleppo, Damascus, and Bagdad, until the 16th of June, 1402, he led 800,000 Mongols against 400,000 of the Turks, under the Sultan Bajazet, son of Amurath. Here met two barbarous nations, two powers for evil which brought nothing but destruction in their train. "The Ottomans were defeated, their sultan taken, and Asia Minor fell into the hands of the conquerors, who did not stop until they came to the deep waters of the Archipelago. The land was theirs, but infidels held the sea. They went in search of other lands to conquer. Taking a survey of Asia from one end to the other, Tamerlane could find but one empire still standing and worthy of his efforts, and that was China. He was leading his countless hordes against that country when finally, March 19, 1405, death stopped the indefatigable old man, who has come down to us as the most terrible personification in history of the evil spirit of conquest. After his death his empire was divided and disappeared."—*Adapted from Duruy.*

Amurath II.—The Ottomans, under Amurath II., again commenced their attacks upon the Venetians in Thessaly, Negropont, and Candia, gaining ground by every assault. "After many combats in Dalmatia, in Servia, in Wallachia, and even in Transylvania, the Hungarians felt the necessity of making a great effort to repulse the Ottoman domination which was coming upon them from three sides at once, along the Adriatic, by the Danube, and across the Carpathian Mountains. A Transylvanian nobleman, named John Hunyadi, was the hero of this war. The White Knight of Wallachia, as he is called, destroyed in the year 1442, 20,000 Turks near Hermanstadt, and some time after he defeated with 15,000 men an army ten times as numerous. He was again victorious in Servia and Bulgaria."

"Meanwhile, the Greek Emperor, in order to gain the help of Catholic Europe, had again offered to subscribe to the union of the two churches. But, if an angel had come down from heaven and said to the Greeks: 'Agree to the union and I will agree to drive out your enemies,' they would have replied: 'Rather Mohammed than the pope.' The union accepted by the emperor was refused by the bishops. It had the effect, however, of instigating a new crusade, which Ladislaw, king of Poland, conducted as far as Bulgaria. The Sultan became uneasy and asked for peace. It was concluded for ten years. He took his oath upon the Koran and Ladislaw upon the Gospels." Against the wishes of Hunyadi, the White Knight of Wallachia, the Crusaders violated the treaty. "Ladislaw was killed, and Hunyadi saved but a small remnant of his army.

"Amurath did not pursue the fugitives. He did not try to attack the great mass of all the Christian nations, whose weight he felt, although he had been victorious over them. He turned his attention to the little powers to the south of the Danube. In 1446 he conquered almost all of Morea and invaded Epirus." There in those inaccessible mountains he found a terrible enemy—George Castriot—called by his countrymen Bey Alexander; by the Turks, Scanderbeg. Amurath had brought him up but he had not been able to erase from the heart of the Christian boy the memory of his fatherland, the faith of his ancestors, and of independence. He threw off the friendship of the Turks and became their most bitter enemy. "In vain did Amurath overrun Albania with his troops; Scanderbeg was always at hand—on their flanks, on their rear, above their heads; always there and always striking, but always out of reach."

Hunyadi, proclaimed regent of Hungary, marched into Servia meeting 150,000 Turks under Amurath. The Hungarian army was almost entirely destroyed; Hunyadi escaped with the greatest difficulty. In 1451 Amurath died at Adrianople, without having conquered Scanderbeg.—*Adapted from Duruy.*

Mohammed II.—Mohammed II. ascended the throne with the resolution of taking Constantinople and of sacrificing everything to that end. "It was his constant thought by day and by night. One morning he called his vizier and said to him: 'Look at my couch; look at this disorder; Constantinople keeps me from closing my eyes. Give me Constantinople.'"

To sound the disposition of his soldiers, Mohammed often wandered through the streets alone and in disguise; and it was fatal to discover the sultan when he wished to escape the vulgar eye. His hours were spent in delineating the plan of the hostile city; in debating with his generals and engineers, on what spot he should erect his batteries, on which side he should assault the walls, where he should spring his mines, to what place he should apply his scaling-ladders."

"He studied with peculiar care the recent discovery of gunpowder, and his artillery surpassed whatever had yet appeared in the world. A Hungarian named Urban,

who was an inventor of cannon, was not favored by the
Greeks, so he deserted to the Moslems. When asked if
he could cast a cannon capable of throwing a ball or
stone of sufficient size to batter the walls of Constantinople, the artist replied: 'I am not ignorant of their
strength, but, were they more solid than those of Baby-
lon, I could oppose an engine of superior power.' On
this assurance a foundry was established at Adrianople,
the metal was prepared, and, at the end of three months,
Urban produced a piece of brass artillery capable of
throwing a stone bullet weighing about six hundred
pounds. A vacant place before the new palace was
chosen for the first experiment; but, to prevent the sudden and mischievous effects of astonishment and fear, a
proclamation was issued, that the cannon would be discharged the ensuing day. The explosion was felt or
heard in the circuit of a hundred furlongs; the ball was
driven above a mile, and on the spot where it fell it
buried itself a fathom deep in the ground. For the con-
veyance of this destructive engine, a frame or carriage of
thirty wagons was linked together, and drawn by a team
of sixty oxen; two hundred men supported the rolling
weight; two hundred and fifty workmen marched before
to smooth the way and prepare the bridges; and nearly
two months were employed in a laborious journey of one
hundred and fifty miles. This enormous engine was
flanked by two cannon of almost equal magnitude. We
may discern the infancy of science when we learn that
the great cannon could be loaded and fired no more than
seven times a day." "A circumstance that distinguished the siege of Constantinople was the union of

ancient and modern artillery. The cannon were intermingled with the mechanical engines for casting stones and darts; the bullet and battering ram were directed against the same walls; nor had the use of gunpowder superseded the use of Greek fire."—*Goodrich.*

Siege of Constantinople.—Mohammed easily found a pretext for declaring war against the Greek Emperor, Constantine Paleologus, and, in the spring of 1453, he led an immense army to beleaguer the city. Two hundred and sixty thousand men surrounded Constantinople, and a fleet was stationed at the entrance to the port, which the besieged had closed with a chain.

"The defense of the city consisted of but 7,000 men, including 2,000 Venetians and Genoese, who were commanded by an able leader, a Genoese named Justiniani. The Emperor Constantine offered up prayers in a church where a Roman bishop was officiating; his court prayed in the others, according to the Greek rites, and a mortal hatred on both sides separated the two parties."—*Duruy.*

Mohammed's troops covered the ground before the landward walls between the Sea of Marmora and the Golden Horn; but he found that even his monster cannon could do but little against the massive fortifications. At length he resolved to assail the city from its weakest side—that facing the Golden Horn. Constantinople is separated from its suburbs, Pera and Galata, by its port, the Golden Horn, an inlet, long and narrow, which extends four miles into the country and is capable of floating 1,200 ships. As the Golden Horn was closed by the chain, Mohammed built a plank road behind the suburbs of the city and connecting the Bosporus with the upper part of the Golden Horn. " The distance was about ten miles; the ground was uneven and overspread with thickets. A level way was covered with a broad platform of strong and solid planks, which they greased to render slippery. Eighty light galleys and brigantines of fifty or thirty oars were drawn upon the shore of the Bosporus, arranged on rollers and transported over the plank road by the power of men and pulleys. The sails were unfurled to the wind and the labor was cheered by song and acclamation. In the course of a single night this Turkish fleet painfully climbed the hill, steered over the plain, and was launched into the shallow waters of the harbor far above the molestation of the deeper vessels of the Greeks.

"After a siege of forty days the fate of Constantinople could no longer be averted. At daybreak, on the 29th of May, the Turks assaulted the city by sea and by land." The Christians offered a desperate resistance, and at first the progress of the besiegers was doubtful. " The Greeks still maintained and improved their advantage, and the voice of the Emperor was heard encouraging his soldiers to achieve, by a last effort, the deliverance of their country. At that fatal moment, the Janizaries arose, fresh, vigorous, and invincible. The Sultan himself, on horseback, with an iron mace in his hand, was the spectator and judge of their valor. He was surrounded by ten thousand of his domestic troops, whom he reserved for the decisive occasion ; and the tide of battle was directed and impelled by his voice and eye. His numerous ministers of justice were posted behind the line, to urge, to restrain, and to punish; and, if danger was in front, shame and inevitable death were in the rear of the fugitives. The cries of fear and of pain were drowned in the martial music of drums, trumpets, and atabals. From the lines, the galleys, and the bridge constructed across the Golden Horn, the Ottoman artillery thundered on all sides; and the camp and city, the Greeks and Turks, were involved in a cloud of smoke, which could only be dispelled by the final deliverance or destruction of the city."—*Goodrich.*

"At eight o'clock in the morning half of Constantinople was taken. Justiniani was mortally wounded; Constantine was dead. By this sacrifice he had ennobled the last hours of the Roman Empire. The other quarters, having their own separate fortifications capitulated."—*Duruy.*

At noon Mohammed rode in triumph into his new capital and went straight to the cathedral of St. Sophia; there before the high altar, where, the preceding night, Constantine had received the Holy Sacrament, he prostrated himself in the Moslem act of worship.

"Sanguinary as Mohammed was, the manner in which he treated the vanquished did him honor. He converted St. Sophia into a Mohammedan mosque, but left the Greeks in possession of several churches. He restrained the fury of his soldiery, gave the Emperor a magnificent funeral, and afterwards made Constantinople a flourishing city."—*Compiled from Goodrich, Duruy and Britannica.* (Further conquests of the Turks, see histories and Britannica under subject: "Turkey;" Origin of the emblem of "Crescent," see "Zigzag Journeys in the Orient.")

Results of Conquest of Constantinople.—The capture of Constantinople by the Venetians in the thirteenth century and by the Turks in the fifteenth century brought loss to the East but gain to the West. The intercourse between the Greek and the Italians brought about a development of art in the cities of Venice, Pisa, and Florence, and many Greek artists became established in Italy. In like manner, the fall of the city before the Turks scattered Greek learning among the Latin and Teutonic races; when Greek libraries were burned and the Greek language proscribed, Greek MSS. of the Bible sedulously copied by the monks of Constantinople from the fifth to the fifteenth century, conveyed the text into Western Europe; the overthrow of the capital of Greek literature, synchronous with the invention of printing, in a great measure caused a revival of learning.—*Adapted from Britannica.* (Effect upon Commerce, see U. S. History. Read "Prince of India," by Lew Wallace.)

V. SPAIN IN THE MIDDLE AGES—*Concluded.*

Christians and Moors.—We have learned that in the eight century Spain was overrun by the Moors from Northern Africa, who drove the Christian Visigoths into the northwestern corner of the peninsula. Here the most resolute of the Christian chiefs found refuge in the Asturian valleys, and not only maintained their freedom, but gradually pushed back the invaders, regaining the land of their fathers. After seven hundred years of almost constant warfare, four Christian kingdoms—Portugal, Aragon, Castile, and Navarre—were firmly established in the peninsula, while the Moorish power had sunk to the single province of Granada.

Washington Irving thus graphically describes life in Spain at this period of the fifteenth century:

"War was the normal state of Granada and its inhabitants; the common people were subject at any moment to be summoned to the field, and all the upper class was a brilliant chivalry. The Christian princes, so successful in regaining the rest of the peninsula, found their triumphs checked at the mountain boundaries of this kingdom. Every peak had its atalaya or watch-tower, ready to make its fire by night or to send up its column of smoke by day, a signal of invasion, at which the whole country was on the alert. To penetrate the defiles of this perilous country, to surprise a frontier fortress, or to make a foray into the vega and a hasty ravage within sight of the very capital, were among the most favorite and daring exploits of the Castilian chivalry. But they never pretended to hold the region thus ravaged; it was sack, burn, plunder, and away! and these desolating inroads were retaliated in kind by the Moorish cavaliers, whose greatest delight was a predatory incursion into the Christian territories beyond the mountains."

The Cid Campeador.—During the long struggle between the Spanish Christians and Mohammedan Moors, there arose many heroes whose wonderful exploits inspired the recital of many fanciful legends. In those days, when two armies met, it was not unusual for one of the bravest knights to ride out of the ranks and challenge a knight on the opposite side to single combat, while the two armies looked on. The one who thus sought to be the champion of his people was called a *challenger*—in Spanish, *campeador*. Though there must have been many of these valiant knights, the Spanish poets of the Middle Ages have attributed all marvelous deeds of virtue and honor that occurred during that period to the one model hero of Spain called "The Cid" (that is, Chief).

Rodrigo Diaz De Bivar, the Cid Campeador, or Lord Champion, was born at Burgos about the year 1025.

When a mere boy he became famous as a campeador by killing a count to avenge an injury done to his father. Ximena, the daughter of the count, first entreated the king for the Cid's death, then won by the splendor of his valor, she herself asked for his hand in marriage. Having aroused the jealousy of the king he was banished and no one was allowed to shelter him under penalty of losing his house and eyes. The Cid finding every door closed against him offered his sword to the Moorish prince of Saragossa, who quickly accepted it, and despatched him to raid the Christian state of Aragon. He and his band of followers rode through Aragon like the wind, slaying every man they met, burning houses and trees, tearing up vines, and stealing what they could carry off.

"After a time he left the employ of the prince of Saragossa, and took service with a Christian count to serve against the Moors. According to the story, he was the most terrible foe they had met." In 1094 he took possession of Valencia after a siege of nine months. He proclaimed himself king, and, it is said, ruled four years with vigor and justice. At length a great Moorish army marched against Valencia and defeated the Cid's army under his favorite lieutenant. The Cid is said to have died of grief at this defeat. According to his last request his body was placed in full armor upon his famous horse, Babieca, and borne in a procession to the church at the monastery of San Pedro, near his native town. Five hundred knights rode as a body-guard, and behind the body followed his wife, Doña Ximena, and her attendants.—*Adapted from Bonner and Britannica.* "The procession moved slowly and silently and the Moors, not quite understanding it, made way for it to pass. It halted at the church at San Pedro, and there, under a canopy which bore the Cid's coat-of-arms, the body was set upright in an ivory chair, still sword in hand." Ten years later, says the legend, the corpse was reverently taken out of the ivory chair and buried before the altar, by the side of the faithful Ximena.

"A whole library of romance and poetry has been written about the Cid. One of the most beautiful stories of his life was written by the English poet, Southey, and called the 'Chronicle of the Cid.'"—*Bonner.* The following poem was written by Felicia Hemans:

THE CID'S DEATH-BED.

It was an hour of grief and fear
　Within Valencia's walls,
When the blue spring heaven lay still and clear
　Above her marble halls.

There were pale cheeks and troubled eyes,
　　And steps of hurrying feet,
Where the Zambra's notes were wont to rise
　　Along the sunny street.

It was an hour of fear and grief
　　On bright Valencia's shore,
For Death was busy with her chief,
　　The noble Campeador.

The Moor king's barks were on the deep,
　　With sounds and signs of war;
But the Cid was passing to his sleep
　　In the silent Alcazar.

No moan was heard through the towers of state,
　　No weeper's aspect seen;
But by the couch Ximena sate
　　With pale though steadfast mien.

Stillness was round the leader's bed,
　　Warriors stood mournful nigh,
And banners o'er his glorious head
　　Were drooping heavily.

And feeble grew the conquering hand,
　　And cold the valiant breast;
He had fought the battles of the land,
　　And his hour was come to rest.

What said the ruler of the field?
　　His voice is faint and low,
The breeze that creeps o'er his lance and shield
　　Hath louder accents now.

"Raise ye no cry, and let no moan
　　Be made when I depart;
The Moor must hear no dirge's tone;
　　Be ye of mighty heart!

"Let the cymbal clash and the trumpet strain;
　　From your walls ring far and shrill,
And fear ye not, for the saints of Spain
　　Shall grant you victory still.

"And gird my form with mail array,
  And set me on my steed;
So go ye forth on your funeral way,
  And God shall give you speed.

"Go with the dead in the front of war,
  All armed with sword and helm,
And march by the camp of King Bucar,
  For the good Castilian realm.

"And let me slumber in the soil
  Which gave my fathers birth;
I have closed my day of battle-toil,
  And my course is done on earth."

Now wave, ye glorious banners, wave!
  Through the lattice a wind sweeps by;
And the arms, o'er the death-bed of the brave,
  Send forth a hollow sigh.

Now wave, ye banners of many a fight,
  As the fresh wind o'er you sweeps;
The wind and the banners fall hushed as night,
  The Campeador—he sleeps!

Sound the battle horn on the breeze of morn,
  And swell out the trumpet's blast
Till the notes prevail o'er the voice of wail,
  For the noble Cid is dead!

(See poems of Spain in Longfellow's "Poems of Places" and Lockhart's "Ancient Spanish Ballads.")

Fall of Granada.—" In 1479 Ferdinand V. became King of Aragon; his wife, Isabella, had previously inherited the sovereignty of Castile and Leon. Thus all the Christian principalities in Spain, except Navarre, were united under one scepter.

" Ferdinand and Isabella administered justice, and restored peace to their dominions, which had long suffered from civil commotions. Filled with a desire to propagate the Christian religion and suppress heresy, these sovereigns introduced the *Inquisition*, a court authorized by the pope to try all persons accused of differing from the established faith. This institution became the terror of Jews and Mohammedans, and even of the Spanish nobles and clergy. On the slightest suspicion they were seized, 'tried' in secrecy, put to the torture to extort a confession of guilt and in many cases given to the flames, while the crown was enriched with their wealth.

"One of the chief events of the reign of Ferdinand and Isabella was the *conquest of Granada*, the last stronghold of the Mohammedans in Spain. For eight months the city, crowded with starving people and distracted by rival factions, held out against an army of seventy thousand. Its luxuriant plain, or *vega*, was the scene of frequent conflicts between the Christian knights and Moorish cavaliers; the feats of valor there performed were long celebrated in the ballads of chivalry. (See chapter entitled "The Last Ravage Before Granada" in Irving's "Granada.")

"Isabella herself, richly attired in complete armor, rode through the camp encouraging her soldiers; while the Moorish ladies toiled upon the ramparts and cheered their defenders with their presence. But famine and insubordination at length compelled the Moslem king to capitulate. He surrendered his capital on condition that the inhabitants should remain undisturbed in their religious faith and in the possession of their property."
—*Quackenbos*.

"The Moorish king, Boabdil, and his principal cavaliers were to perform the act of homage and take an oath of fealty to the Castilian crown. To Boabdil was secured, his wealthy estates, both in and out of Granada, and the lordship of various towns, lands, and fertile valleys in the Alpuxarras, forming a petty sovereignty."—*Irving*.

"Thus terminated in 1492 the Saracen Empire in Spain, after an existence of nearly eight centuries.

"The Moors were for a time allowed freedom of worship, but they were in the sixteenth century compelled to embrace Christianity or leave the country. Thousands departed from their native land, and those who remained lived in constant dread of the cruelties of the Inquisition. By such intolerance Spain lost multitudes of her most useful and thrifty inhabitants."—*Quackenbos*.

The Last Sigh of the Moor.—"Having rejoined his family, Boabdil set forward with a heavy heart for his allotted residence in the valley of the Purchena. At two leagues' distance, the cavalcade, winding into the skirts of the Alpuxaras, ascended an eminence commanding the last view of Granada. As they arrived at this spot. the Moors paused involuntarily to take a farewell gaze at their beloved city, which a few steps more would shut from their sight forever. Never had it appeared so lovely in their eyes. The sunshine, so bright in that transparent climate, lit up each tower and minaret, and rested gloriously upon the crowning battlements of the Alhambra; while the vega spread its enameled bosom of verdure below, glistening with the silver windings of the Xenil. The Moorish cavaliers gazed with a silent agony of tenderness and grief upon that delicious abode, the scene of their loves and pleasures. While they yet looked, a light cloud of smoke burst forth from the citadel, and presently a peal of artillery, faintly heard, told that the city was taken possession of, and the throne of the Moslem kings was lost forever. The heart of Boabdil, softened by misfortunes, and overcharged with grief, could no longer contain itself. 'Allah Achbar! God is great!" said he; but the words of resignation died upon his lips, and he burst into tears.

"His mother, the intrepid Ayxa, was indignant at his weakness. ' You do well,' said she, ' to weep like a woman for what you failed to defend like a man.' * * *

"The hill upon which they stood took the name of ' Feg Allah Achbar ;' but the point of view, commanding the last prospect of Granada, is known among Spaniards by the name of ' El ultimo suspiro del Moros ', or 'The last sigh of the Moor.'" * * *

How the Castilian Monarchs Took Possession of Granada.—"It was on the 6th of January, 1492, that the sovereigns made their triumphal entry with grand military parade into the city of Granada." * * *

"The royal procession advanced to the principal mosque, which had been consecrated as a cathedral. Here the sovereigns offered up prayers and thanksgivings, and the choir of the royal chapel chanted a triumphal anthem, in which they were joined by all the courtiers and cavaliers." * * *

" When the religious ceremonies were concluded, the court ascended to the stately palace of the Alhambra, and entered by the great Gate of Justice. The halls lately occupied by turbaned infidels now rustled with stately dames and Christian courtiers, who wandered with eager curiosity over this far-famed palace, admiring its verdant courts and gushing fountains, its halls decorated with elegant arabesques and storied with inscriptions, and the splendor of its gilded and brilliantly painted ceilings." * * *

"The Spanish sovereigns fixed their throne in the presence-chamber of the palace, so long the seat of Moorish royalty. Hither the inhabitants of Granada repaired, to pay them homage and kiss their hands in token of vassalage; and their example was followed by deputies from all the towns and fortresses of the Alpuxaras, which had not hitherto submitted.

"Thus terminated the war of Granada, after ten years of incessant fighting; equaling the far-famed siege of Troy in duration, and ending, like that, in the capture of the city. Thus ended also the dominion of the Moors in Spain, having endured seven hundred and seventy-eight years from the memorable defeat of Roderick, the last of the Goths, on the banks of the Guadalete."—*Irving.*

TOWARD THE SEA.

There was weeping in Granada on that eventful day;
One king in triumph entered in; one, vanquished, rode away.
Down from the Alhambra's minarets was every crescent flung
And the cry of "Santiago!" through the jeweled palace rung.
    And singing, singing, singing,
    Were the nightingales of Spain,
    But the Moorish monarch, lonely,
    The cadences heard only.
    "They sadly sing," said he:
    "They sadly sing to me."
    And through the groves melodious
    He rode toward the sea.

There was joy in old Granada on that eventful day:
One king in triumph entered in; one slowly rode away.
Up the Alcala singing marched the gay cavaliers
Gained was the Moslem Empire of twice three hundred years;
    And singing, singing, singing,
    Were the nightingales of Spain,
    But the Moorish monarch lonely,
    The cadences heard only.
    "They sadly sing," said he,
    "They sadly sing to me,
    All the birds of Andalusia!"
    And he rode toward the sea.

Through the groves of Alpuxaras, on that eventful day,
The vanquished king rode slowly and tearfully, away.
He paused upon the Xenil, and saw Granada fair
Wreathed with the sunset's roses in palpitating air.
    And singing, singing, singing,
    Were the nightingales of Spain.
    But the Moorish monarch, lonely,
    The cadences heard only.
    "They sadly sing," said he,
    "They sadly sing to me;
    Oh, groves of Andalusia!"
    He rode toward the sea.

The Vega heaped with flowers below the city lay,
And faded in the sunset, as he slowly rode away,
And he paused again a moment amid the cavaliers,
And saw the golden palace shine through the mist of tears;
    And singing, singing, singing,
    Were the nightingales of Spain.
    But the Moorish monarch, lonely,
    The cadences heard only.
    "They sadly sing," said he,
    "They sadly sing to me;
    Farewell, O Andalusia!"
    And he rode toward the sea.

Past the gardens of Granada rode Isabella fair,
As twilight's parting roses fell on the sea of air;
She heard the lisping fountains, and not the Moslem's sighs
She saw the sun-crowned mountains, and not the tear-wet eyes.
      "Sing on," she said, "forever,
        O nightingales of Spain;
        Xenil nor Guadalquivir
        Will *he* ne'er see again.
      Ye sweetly sing," said she,
      "Ye sweetly sing to me."
        She rode toward the palace;
        He rode toward the sea.

" I see above yon palace your pinnacles of gems
The banners of the chalice, the dual diadems:
It fills my heart with rapture, as from a smile divine,
I feel the will to bless it, if all the world were mine.
      "Sing on," she said, "forever,
        O nightingales of Spain;
        Xenil nor Guadalquivir
        Will he ne'er see again.
      Ye sweetly sing," said she,
      "Ye sweetly sing to me."
        She rode toward the capital;
        He rode toward the sea.
                        -*Butterworth.*

c. 1896
LIST OF WORKS

Which, by kind permission of the publishers or authors (where copyright is in force), are quoted from or referred to in this work.

DRURY'S "Middle Ages," translated by E. & M. Whitney, edited by George D. Adams, and published by Henry Holt & Co.
MYERS' "General History," by Ginn & Co.
LYDIA HOYT FARMER'S "Boys' Book of Famous Rulers," by Thomas Crowell & Co.
BONNER'S "Child's History of Spain," Copyright, 1894, by Harper & Brothers.
BONNER'S "Child's History of France," Copyright, 1893, by Harper & Brothers.
GOODRICH'S "History of England," by E. H. Butler & Co.
CHARLOTTE YONGE'S "History of Germany," by D. Lothrop & Co.
CHARLOTTE YONGE'S "History of France," by Estes & Lauriat.
LEW WALLACE'S "Ben Hur" and "Prince of India," by Harper & Brothers.
QUACKENBOS' "School History of the World," by D. Appleton & Co. 1876.
DICKENS' "Child's History of England."
BUTTERWORTH'S "Zigzag Journeys," by Estes & Lauriat.
IRVING'S "Granada" and "Alhambra."
EMERTON'S "Introduction to Study of Middle Ages," by Ginn & Co.
EDGAR'S "Crusades and Crusaders," by Ward, Lock & Bowden.
GIBBON'S "Decline and Fall of the Roman Empire."
CHURCH'S "Stories from English History," by the Macmillan Co.
PETER PARLEY'S "Cabinet Library," 1849.
RIDPATH'S "History of the World," by Jones Brothers Publishing Company.
"ENCYCLOPEDIA BRITANNICA."
BARNES' "General History," by American Book Company.
JANE ANDREW'S "Ten Boys."
SCOTT'S "Ivanhoe" and "Talisman."
MISS KIRKLAND'S "History of France" and "History of England."
MARY MAPES DODGE'S "Hans Brinker."
JANE PORTER'S "Scottish Chiefs."
GRACE AGUILAR'S "Days of Bruce."
LONGFELLOW'S "Poems of Europe."
LOCKHART'S "Ancient Spanish Ballads."
BUTTERWORTH'S Poem "Towards the Sea."
FELICIA HEMANS' "Homes of England," "The Cid's Deathbed" and "The Alhambra."
BULWER LYTTON'S "The Last Crusader."
OTHER POEMS from Goldsmith, Thomson, N. P. Willis and Emanuel Geibel.
REFERENCES to Lowell's "Sir Launfal," Tennyson's "King Arthur," Bryant's "William Tell," Knowles' "William Tell," James Montgomery's "Arnold Winkelried."

www.ingramcontent.com/pod-product-compliance
Lightning Source LLC
Chambersburg PA
CBHW032130160426
43197CB00008B/588